Dialectical Materialism

Henri Lefebvre

Translated from the French by
John Sturrock

JONATHAN CAPE
THIRTY BEDFORD SQUARE
LONDON

This translation first published November 1968
Reprinted 1969 and 1970
© 1968 by Jonathan Cape Ltd
Translated from the French *Le Matérialisme Dialectique*
© 1940 by Presses Universitaires de France

Jonathan Cape Ltd, 30 Bedford Square, London WC1

Paperback ISBN 0 224 61506 8
Hardback ISBN 0 224 61507 6

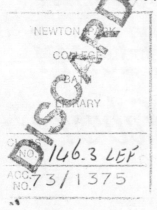
Condition of Sale

Printed and bound in Great Britain
by Richard Clay (The Chaucer Press), Ltd
Bungay, Suffolk

Contents

TRANSLATOR'S NOTE 7

CODE TO REFERENCES 9

FOREWORD TO THE FIFTH EDITION 13

I. THE DIALECTICAL
CONTRADICTION 21
A critique of Hegel's dialectic 46
Historical materialism 60
Dialectical materialism 79
Unity of the doctrine 100

II. THE PRODUCTION OF MAN 114
Analysis of the Product 119
The activities of integration 124
The controlled sector and the uncontrolled
sector 132
Physical determinism 141
Social determinism 145
The total man 148
Towards the total content 166

SELECTED BIBLIOGRAPHY 169

A NOTE ON THE AUTHOR 171

TRANSLATOR'S NOTE

Professor Lefebvre's text contains many references to the writings of Hegel and Marx, and where possible the source of these is given in the form of a note in the text itself. Since the original French edition of *Le Matérialisme dialectique* refers only to specific works, and not to specific editions of these works, and since also Professor Lefebvre's own papers relating to the book were destroyed during the 1939–45 war, we have simply carried over the references as they are given in the French edition from which the translation was made.

CODE TO REFERENCES

Hegel : ED = Erste Druckschriften

E = Enzyklopädie der philosophischen Wissenschaften (tr. Encyclopaedia of the Philosophical Sciences)

GP = Geschichte der Philosophie (tr. History of Philosophy)

P = Phänomenologie des Geistes (tr. The Phenomenology of Mind)

PR = Philosophie des Rechts (tr. The Philosophy of Right)

WL = Wissenschaft der Logik (tr. Science of Logic)

Marx : DI = Die deutsche Ideologie (tr. German Ideology)

HF = Die heilige Familie (tr. The Holy Family)

K = Das Kapital (tr. Capital)

KPO = Zur Kritik der politischen Ökonomie (tr. Critique of Political Economy)

M = Ökonomische-philosophische Manuskripte (1844, 1857–8)

Man = Manifest der kommunistischen Partei (tr. The Communist Manifesto)

MP = La Misère de la philosophie (tr. The Poverty of Philosophy)

N = Nachlass

The life of the Spirit is not that life which shrinks from death and seeks to keep itself clear of all corruption, but rather the life which endures the presence of death within itself and preserves itself alive within death.

Hegel, *The Phenomenology of Mind*

FOREWORD TO THE FIFTH EDITION

This little book represents an episode in the fierce struggle inside (and outside) Marxism between the dogmatists and the critique of dogmatism. This struggle is not over; it goes bitterly on. Dogmatism is strong, it can call on the force of authority, of the State and its institutions. Moreover, it has advantages: it is simple and easily taught; it steers clear of complex problems, this being precisely the aim and meaning of dogmatism; it gives its adherents a feeling of both vigorous affirmation and security.

When this book was written, almost twenty-five years ago now [1961], official or 'institutional' Marxism was already veering towards a systematic philosophy of Nature. There was a tendency to look on philosophy, in the name of the 'positive' sciences and especially physics, as a framework in which to bring together the results of these sciences and so obtain a definitive picture of the world. Among the ruling circles, under the influence of Stalin and Zhdanov, there was a desire to merge philosophy with the natural sciences in this way by 'basing' the dialectical method on the dialectic in Nature.

Why this systematization? Today, although not everything is yet clear, we are beginning to see and know better what took place:

1. A deep mistrust prevailed (it still does) with regard to Marx's early writings. The ideological authorities in the Marxist and communist workers' movement feared – not without cause – that Marx's

13

thought would be understood quite differently if these newly published works were read. As politicians, operating in accordance with those methods of political action and organization which they practised, they forestalled them; they made their dogmatism more rigid so as to protect it against the impact and preserve it.

At the precise moment when hitherto disregarded concepts were being rediscovered (alienation, praxis, the total man and social totality, etc.), and when those who had read the young Marx were clearing the way for the rediscovery of Hegel, the dogmatists were moving in an opposite direction. They became more contemptuous than ever of Hegel and Hegelianism, they rejected Marx's early writings as being tainted with idealism and as having preceded the formulation of dialectical materialism, they drew a line between Marx and his predecessors and another between the so-called philosophical and so-called scientific works in the Marxian corpus, they fetishized certain texts by Stalin, especially the notorious theoretical chapter in the *History of the Communist Party of the U.S.S.R.*, etc.

2. From this there evolved a simplified Marxism and materialism, reduced to a recognition of the practical and material world 'as it is', without addition or interpretation. Its methodology also contracted. In spite of explicit 'classic' passages in Marx, Engels and Lenin, the official Marxists contested the validity of formal logic, as having come from Aristotle and from the ideological 'superstructures' of ancient or medieval society. Henceforth the laws of the dialectic could be taught as laws of Nature, by leaving out the mediation of logic and discourse and

thus passing over the problems which this mediation poses.

It is interesting to note that this simplified ontology of material Nature followed other simplifications no less unwarranted. For quite a long period – that of the great economic crisis of 1929–33 and its aftermath – Marxism had been reduced to a single science: political economy. It had become an economicism. The dogmatists of this persuasion cheerfully rejected the other sciences of the human reality: sociology, as being tainted with reformism, and psychology, as being irredeemably bourgeois. Within this simplification regrettable factions had already appeared: one which subjected theory to the demands of the practical instruction of the young, another which subjected it to the imperatives of the political situation of the moment. Theory was turned either into an ideological tool or into the superstructure of a particular society. It was deprived of any depth, in the interests of a utilitarianism at once constricted and robust. Thus, during the period when specifically economic problems were uppermost (crises in capitalist countries and the start of planning in the U.S.S.R.), economicism flourished.

3. But there is another, worse, aspect to this transformation of Marxism into a philosophy of Nature: it was a massive exercise in diversion. While they were holding forth about waves and corpuscles and the 'continuous-discontinuous' objective dialectic and debating these 'freely', the crucial issues were being lost to view. What was really at stake was no longer in the forefront of people's minds, which had been led as far away as possible, into the depths of Nature and cosmological speculation. Stalin and the Stalinists

15

were adept at employing these diversionary tactics. The 'Democratic Constitution' was solemnly promulgated in 1936, after the murder of Kirov (we now know, thanks to N. Khrushchev, that it was Stalin who instigated this), at precisely the same moment as the terror was being unleashed. The systemization of dialectical materialism into a scientific philosophy of Nature dates from the same period and pursues the same objective: to hide the real theoretical and practical problems.

It is perfectly possible to accept and uphold the thesis of the dialectic in Nature; what is inadmissible is to accord it such enormous importance and make it the criterion and foundation of dialectical thought.

4. For many and obscure reasons institutional Marxism refuses to listen to talk of *alienation*. It either rejects the concept or accepts it only with reservations and provisos. The dogmatists see it merely as a staging-post in Marx's thought, quickly superseded on the one hand by his discovery of dialectical materialism as a philosophy and on the other by his formulation of a scientific political economy (*Capital*). To them it seems misguided to bring back the concept of alienation, independently of any idealist systemization, so as to make use of it in the critical analysis of 'reality' and incorporate it in the categories of the social sciences (especially sociology). Or so at least they pretend. Why? Obviously for political reasons which are both short-term and short-sighted. We cannot confine the use of the concept of alienation to the study of bourgeois societies. It may enable us to uncover and criticize numerous forms of alienation (of women, of colonial or ex-colonial countries, of work and the worker, of

'consumer societies', of the bourgeoisie itself in the society it has fashioned in accordance with its own self-interest, etc.), but it also enables us to uncover and criticize ideological and political alienations inside socialism, particularly during the Stalinist period. Institutional Marxists choose to reject the concept so as to avoid such risks and blunt its cutting edge.

There is no need to stress that I was not fully aware of these related problems when I wrote this book. Nevertheless, it takes as its axis the dialectical movements within the human and social reality. In the foreground it places the concept of alienation, as a philosophical concept and an analytical tool, not the dialectic in Nature. It ignores the systematized philosophy of the material object. The concluding and fundamental chapter, 'The Production of Man', rejects popular economicism and sociologism as well as the stress that has been laid on non-human materiality. Which is to say that, as it stands, it is tainted only very slightly with dogmatism, and that the author does not hesitate to allow it once again, with all its weaknesses, to be read and criticized.

The fact remains that today we can and must re-read Marx with fresh eyes, especially the early works, which it is wrong to call 'philosophical' since they contain a radical critique of all systematic philosophy. 'The becoming-philosophy of the world is at the same time a becoming-world of philosophy, its realization is also its destruction,' Marx wrote at the time when he was drafting his doctoral thesis on *The Philosophy of Nature in Democritus and Epicurus*. In this thesis he shows that there is a dialectical movement inside each of the philosophical systems he examines – a dialectical movement in their mutual contradiction, and finally, in each of them, the objectification of a particular form of consciousness which can be defined only through its relation to the real world and the social praxis in that real world (in this case Greek society). Philosophy as such, as the constantly renewed and constantly misleading attempt to systematize and to formulate a satisfactory image of man or of human satisfaction, disintegrates. It is right to take what it proposes into account but only in order to realize it, a realization which poses new problems.

In what was almost the very next thing he wrote Marx sets out to take critical stock of Hegelianism and shows how this perfect systemization disintegrates. Two attitudes or camps resulted from this in Germany. One wanted 'to abolish philosophy without realizing it', as being a theoretical formulation of man's achievement, the other thought that 'philosophy could be realized without abolishing it', as being a merely theoretical and abstract formulation of man, his freedom and his achievement. The mission of the proletariat in Germany, but not only in Germany, was above all to transcend philosophy, that is to realize it by abolishing it as such. 'Just as philosophy finds its material weapons in the proletariat, so does the proletariat find its intellectual weapons in philosophy ... Philosophy is the head of this emancipation, the proletariat is its heart. Philosophy cannot be realized without the abolition of the proletariat, the proletariat cannot be abolished unless philosophy is realized.' [M]

Marx never returned to this theory of the *transcending* of philosophy as such, taken, that is, in its entire development, from the Greeks to Hegel, either to refute or reject it. In modern-day terms, which are not those of Marx, we can say that for him philosophy was of a *programmatic* nature. It has provided and still does provide man with a programme or, if one prefers, a project. This programme or project must be brought face to face with reality, that is with the praxis (social practice), a confrontation which introduces new elements and poses problems other than those of philosophy.

This theory was integrated into Marxism, since Marx's thought proceeded by way of successive extensions or integrations to wholes, or (partial) totalities which were increasingly extensive as well as increasingly close to the praxis. No element or 'moment' is lost. In particular, the moment of the radical critique and of negativity (which includes the critique of religion, philosophy and the State in general) finds a place in this development and is not resorbed in the interests of a pure and simple 'positivity'. Marx's thought therefore cannot be reduced either to the positivist attitude which sends philosophy back into a past that is over and done with, or to the attitude of those who perpetuate philosophical system-building.

At a time when dogmatism is crumbling and dissolving, the early writings of Marx become of the first importance. They enable us to reinstate the problems raised by his ideas and by Marxism, problems which are still fundamentally our own ones.

HENRI LEFEBVRE

Paris
December 1961

I

THE DIALECTICAL
CONTRADICTION

Formal logic seeks to determine the workings of the intellect independently of the experimental, and hence particular and contingent, content of every concrete assertion. Formalism is justified by the requirement of universality. Formal logic studies purely analytical transformations, inferences in which thought is concerned only with itself. The only value which any definite assertion has for the logician is as an example to teach by; these examples or pretexts are interchangeable. Once posited, thought moves within itself, with a minimum of content, ever ready to rid itself of this content and never acquiring any new content; it thus runs no risk of error. This formal thinking obeys only its pure identity with itself: 'A is A. If A is B and B is C, then A is C.' 'In formal logic the movement of thought seems to be something separate, which has nothing to do with the object being thought,' says Hegel. [GP]

If this independence of content and form were attained it would either forbid the form being applied to any particular content, or else allow it to be applied to any content whatsoever, even an irrational one. Moreover, is it conceivable that there should be two completely separate logics, the one abstract, a logic of pure form, and the other concrete, a logic of content? In point of fact formal logic never manages to do without the content; it may break a piece off this content and reduce it, or make it more and more 'abstract', but it can never free itself from it entirely. It works on determinate judgments, even if it does see their content simply as an excuse for applying the form. As Hegel points out, a completely simple, void identity cannot even be formulated. When the logician who has just posited 'A' posits 'not-A', and asserts that 'A is not not-A', he is adopting the form of negation without having justified it; he is thus positing the 'other' of A, the difference or non-identity, and is even positing a third term, 'A', which is neither 'plus A' nor 'minus A'. The term 'not-A' is posited only to vanish, but in this way identity becomes a negation of the negation, a distinction within a relation. Therefore the logical principles (of identity and non-contradiction) are not purely analytical. Moreover, as soon as we posit a determinate judgment (for example: the tree is green) we are positing 'A is B'; we do not remain within the identity and formal repetition, but introduce a content, a difference, in relation to which formal identity is also a difference. [WL II]

On the one hand formal logic is always related to the content, and thus preserves a certain concrete significance; on the other it has always been linked to a general assertion about that content, that is to an ontology, or a dogmatic and metaphysical theme. Logical theories of the real, as Hegel remarks ironically, have always been much too soft-hearted towards things, they have busied themselves rooting out contradictions from the real only to carry them over into the mind and there leave them unresolved. The objective world thus comes to be made up ultimately of isolated and immobile facts, of essences, substances or parts, which are external one to another. These essences are what they are, the theory of identity having been applied unreservedly, and that is all that can be said about them.

Most often the logic of identity has been linked with the metaphysic of Being.[1] Identity is seen not as a pure form but as an internal, essential and objective property of Being. From the identity within thought we can move on to objective identity, which characterizes the existence of every real substance. Being – and each being – is identical to itself and thus defines itself. Identity is therefore taken as both form and content: its own content. This aspect of Aristotelianism (the most abstract and least profound perhaps, if it is true that Aristotelianism was also a theory of the individuality of every concrete being) was isolated and developed by later philosophies. Up till Leibniz the western mind was engaged on an heroic but vain attempt to extract the content from the form, to pass logically from thought Being to existent Being, that is to deduce the world.

The relationship between content and form in formal logic is therefore ill-defined and debatable. Formal logic preserves both too much and too little content. This content is one-sided, it is in point of fact received, then separated, immobilized and metaphysically transposed. The logico-metaphysical postulate is precisely the same as that of the 'magical' mentality: the relationship between form and content is seen

[1] It is sometimes bound up with a metaphysical atomism (Dühring), with a theory of spiritual structure (Husserl) or an ontology of sensation (physicalism of the Vienna School), but it is never free of a dogmatism which realizes a limited part of the content.

as a participation. Formal identity becomes a schema of identification in this 'magical' sense. Formal logic does not achieve its aim when it is turned against magical doctrines and mysticisms, it does not really transcend theories that are devoid of rational rigour and so remains on their level.

It leaves open an essential problem, and poses an exigency: how are the form and content to be united? Since formalism fails to do this, should we not reverse the order and go from the content to the form instead of from the form to the content?

Formal logic has involved rational thought in a series of conflicts. The first is a conflict between rigour and fruitfulness. In the syllogism (even if it is not totally sterile) thought is rigorously coherent only if it keeps within the repetition of the same terms. It is well known that the induction which enables us to move on from facts to laws is not a rigorous one. Every fact, everything that is established experimentally, introduces into thought an element that is new and hence without necessity from the point of view of logical formalism. The sciences have developed outside formal logic or even in opposition to it; but then, if science is fruitful it does not start from necessary truths, nor follow a rigorous development. Logic and philosophy remain outside the sciences, or only follow after them, in order to establish their specific methods; they contribute nothing of their own. Conversely, the sciences are external to philosophy, either below or above it, and their methods of discovery have nothing to do with rigorous logic. The scientist proves that thought is mobile by advancing into knowledge, but the philosopher gets his revenge by calling into question the value of science. The conflict between rigour and fruitfulness spreads, giving rise to the problem of knowledge and of the value of science.

Secondly, if Being is what it is and never anything else, if every idea is either absolutely true or false absolutely, the real contradictions between existence and thought are excluded from thought. What, in things and in consciousness, is diverse and fluid is relinquished to the dialectic in the old sense of the term : to imprecise argument and to the games of the sophist or the advocate, who can please himself whether he pleads for or against. If thought is defined by identity, then it is also defined by immobility. Hence a fresh conflict develops between the structure of the understanding and mobility, between the coherence of clear thinking and the different polarities and shifting forces of actual experience. Reason is located outside the real, in the ideal. Logic becomes the concern of a fictive being, pure thought, for whom the real will seem impure. Conversely, the real finds itself being rejected and handed over to the irrational.

When Hegel set out on his philosophical career he found Reason, which is thought in its most highly developed form, profoundly rent by these internal conflicts. Kantian dualism had aggravated them to the point where they became intolerable, by deliberately dissociating form from content, thought from the 'thing-in-itself', and the faculty of knowing from the object of knowledge. Hegel's purpose was to resolve these conflicts, and to repossess, in their movement, all the elements of philosophical thought and of the mind, which had reached him in a state of dislocation and dissension.

This aim in itself embraced the method and the central idea of Hegelian doctrine: the consciousness of an infinitely rich unity of thought and reality, of form and content, a necessary unity, implied in thought's internal conflicts, since every conflict is a relation, yet one which has got to be fought for and determined by transcending the 'one-sided' terms that have come into conflict.

At the time when Hegel was being born to the life of the mind, great events (the Revolutionary period, great national wars, the Napoleonic period; as well as the growth of science and of the historical spirit, the break-up of feudal society and the appearance of a new civilization) were making it necessary to draw up a vast balance-sheet of culture, to attempt a 'synthesis' of all these diverse elements.

As far as the search for a method was concerned, the problem facing Hegel was many-sided. In the first place, the art of argument and controversy had to be integrated with precise thinking. Argument is inconclusive and uncertain unless it is directed by a mind already sure of itself. But argument is also free and alive, moving in the midst of theses and terms that are diverse, fluid and contradictory. There is a good side to the scepticism to which endless argument leads: it shows that 'when, in any proposition whatsoever, one isolates its reflexive aspect, it is necessarily revealed that the concepts have either been transcended or else that they are linked in such a way as to contradict one another ...' [ED] Scepticism is useful in that it introduces the negative element into thought, it 'dissolves' the limited and contradictory representations that the understanding (which has the fundamental power of 'positing' an assertion) always tends to posit as absolutes, by bringing them into collision with each other. The understanding takes itself to be the absolute, whereas it is only a limited, momentary and, so to speak, provisional power; it is thus involved in antinomies. The 'right' scepticism criticizes and destroys common dogmatism.

In a real-life argument there is something true in every idea. Nothing is wholly or 'indisputably' true, nothing is absolutely absurd or false. By comparing theses thought spontaneously seeks a higher unity. Each thesis is false in what it asserts absolutely but true in what it asserts relatively (its content); and it is true in what it denies relatively (its well-founded criticism of the other thesis) and false in what it denies absolutely (its dogmatism).

But this dialectic must be uprooted from sophistry, which tends out of pure vanity to break up what is true and solid and leads to no conclusions save that of the vanity of the object treated dialectically. [WL III] Sophistry accepts unfounded presuppositions, it oscillates between Being and Nothingness, between the true and the false taken in isolation. 'We give the name of dialectic to that higher movement of the reason in which these absolutely separate appearances pass into one another ... and in which the presupposition is transcended.' [WL I] Once it is linked to a precise consciousness of the movement of thought the dialectic takes on a new and higher meaning. It becomes a technique, an art and a science : a technique of argument controlled and orientated from within towards a rational coherence; an art of analysing the multiple aspects and relations of words and things, without destroying their essence; a science

27

which releases whatever is true in all the contradictory ideas between which the common understanding oscillates.

Hegel next needed to rescue logic, the definite form by means of which thought contains something solid. To achieve this he had to find the link between the form and a reality both fluid and diverse, and, consequently, to transform the form of traditional logic. He needed to start not from this form but from the content, that 'rich content' which was so diverse and contradictory but which had already been worked on through thousands of years of human activity. The task was feasible; this content 'is already thought, universal thought', since it is both consciousness and knowledge. The form of logic is part of it, in fact it is that element of it which has been most fully developed.

In Hegel's philosophy the human Mind therefore proposes to repossess all its 'objective products' [E §572] in every sphere: art, religion, social life, science and history. It seeks to raise them to their most conscious form – the form of a concept – by transcending everything which divides and disperses the content, or externalizes it in relation to rational thought. This content is given, consisting as it does of multiple representations: desires, material objects, impressions or intuitions, Nature, human experience. From this 'raw material' the notions that are 'immersed' in it have got to be extracted. The content was substantial, but outside thought, while rigorous thought remained motionless and empty. We must, says the *Phenomenology*, 'tear away the veil from substantial life' and raise it to the highest degree of rationality.

To this end Reason itself must be defined by the movement of thought which challenges, unseats and dissolves particular assertions and limited contents, which passes from one to the other and tends to dominate them. Thus the dialectic, the immediate relation between thought and its diverse, fluid content, is no longer outside logic. It is integrated with logic, which it transforms by transforming itself. It becomes the life and internal movement of thought: both content and form. 'The understanding determines and perseveres in its determinations; reason is dialectical because it dissolves the determinations of the understanding; it is positive because it produces the universal and includes in it the particular,' says the *Introduction to the Greater Logic*. Hegelianism thus raises itself to the highest consciousness, to the unity of the discursive understanding and the reflective reason, to intelligent reason and rational understanding.

There is no object in which a contradiction cannot be found, that is two necessary and conflicting determinations, 'an object without contradictions being nothing more than a pure abstraction of the understanding, which maintains one of these determinations with a sort of violence and conceals from consciousness the contrary determination that contains the first one ... ' [E §89] In this way the negative moment, which sophistry, scepticism and the old form of dialectic isolated and turned against logical thought, finds its place and its function. It expresses the movement of the content, 'the immanent soul of the content' which is transcended, no element of it being self-sufficient or able to remain enclosed within itself.

The negative is equally a positive; whatever is contradicted is not reduced to a zero, to an abstract nothingness, but essentially to the negation of its particular content; in other words such a negation is not a complete negation but the negation of the determinate thing which is being dissolved, and therefore a determinate negation. The result, being a determinate negation, has a content; it is a new concept, but higher and richer than the previous one, having been enriched by its negation or, in other words, its contrary; it contains the other but is also more than the other, it is their unity ... [WL I]

It is the dialectic of the content which causes it to progress.

Kant had opened up a new path for logic. He had drawn a distinction between analytical judgments (formally rigorous but sterile) and synthetic judgments (without which thought can advance but only by acknowledging a contingent fact). He was seeking to demonstrate the existence of judgments which were both fruitful and rigorous, and necessary without being tautologous: synthetic *a priori* judgments. In synthesis he had already hoped to find the principle of unity between rigour and fruitfulness. But he saw his synthetic *a priori* judgments as pure, empty forms, separated from their content, as instruments of cognition indifferent in relation to their subject-matter, as subjective in relation to the object – as still conforming therefore to traditional formalism. According to Hegel this dualism must be transcended.

If they are developed (and profoundly modified)

Kant's ideas prove infinitely fertile. They turn into a new logic. Hegel did not discover contradiction; he insists on the fact that all thought and all philosophy, even when it opts for one of the opposed terms by striving to reduce or exclude the other, moves amongst contradictions. The 'dialectical moment', that expedient of the mind which finds itself obliged to move from a position it had hoped was definitive and to take account of something further, thereby denying its original assertion, is to be found everywhere, in every age, although not properly elucidated. Hegel discovered the Third Term, which results once any determination has been enriched by its negation and transcended; it is produced rigorously whenever two terms are in contradiction, yet it is a new moment of Being and of thought.

Hegelian Reason proceeds completely rigorously, by determining the third term whenever there is an internal contradiction. It thus brings into being the determinations and categories of thought. The synthesis ceases to be an *a priori* one, immobilized, fixed and come from who knows where. The Kantian table of categories was both formal and empirical, and Kant attached these categories arbitrarily to the unity of transcendental apperception, to the abstract 'I', without having demonstrated their necessary and internal unity. Hegel will strive to demonstrate the immanent unity of the categories and to produce them, from a starting-point purified from every formal or empirical presupposition; he will generate them out of a wholly internal movement of the mind, a rigorous yet progressive sequence in which each determination emerges from its predecessors by way of opposition and resolution – by a synthesis.

The notion of the Third Term reacts decisively on the notion of contradiction, which ceases to be an absurdity, a hesitation and an oscillation or confusion of thought. The 'necessary' conflict between finite determinations is 'brought to light'; the relation between the contradictory terms is lucidly established. In the content and the form of thought, movement has an antagonistic structure. The Becoming passes through the conflicting terms, confronts each of them, on its own level and in its own degree, with its 'other', which is in conflict with it, and finally transcends their opposition by creating something new.

Nothingness is, but only relatively, within Being itself, within each being and each degree of Being, as its 'other' or specific negation. The thought of Nothingness in general is merely the thought of Being in general, Being as isolated or 'in-itself', which is instantly seen to be void and insufficient. Being is not, non-Being is; they are by virtue of each other. In thought as in reality they pass into one another all the time, and are thus set in motion and enter into the Becoming, or 'Being which remains in itself within Nothingness'. The Becoming in general is the Third Term, born from the contradiction whose first term is Being stripped of all content and hence without presuppositions. This unity is attained through a synthesis and yet it is an analysis or deduction, because it posits what had been implied in the notion. [E §88]

Conversely, the Becoming in general is primary, determinate existence, the primary and concrete, of which pure Being and Nothingness are the abstract moments. The Becoming is a becoming of something, of a being; and within the Becoming nothingness is the end of whatever is, a passing and transition into something else; it is a limit and a passing away as well as a creation, a possibility and a birth. Once they are joined dialectically abstractions regain the concrete, and return into that fluid unity which had been broken by the abstractive understanding. There is nothing in heaven or earth which does not contain within it Being and Nothingness. [WL I] The end of a thing, its limit, the term towards which it tends by virtue of its inner nature, hence also its 'beyond', all form part of that thing. 'The being of a finite thing is to have in its inner being as such the seed of its passing away; the hour of its birth is also the hour of its death.' [WL II]

For the assertion posited initially and immediately, every negation is thus the start of fresh determinations. In Being and in thought negativity is creative, it is the root of movement and the pulse of life. No reality can remain 'in itself', that is isolated and detached, protected from the Becoming and immobile in the possession of Being – its own being. Every determinate existence is a relation : 'A determinate, finite being is a being necessarily related to another being; it is a content in a necessary relation with another content, with the whole world … ' [WL II] Each determinate existence is thus involved in the total movement and obliged to emerge from itself. It is what it is, yet at its very core it has the infinite within it. In its determination it is a being determined not to be what it is, i.e. not to remain what it is. [WL II] The 'other', the second term, is equally as real as the first, it is on the same plane, at the same level or degree of reality and in the same 'sphere' of thought. It negates, makes manifest and completes the first term, by expressing its one-sidedness. The two terms act and react on each other; to call a halt is impossible. The negation negates itself, and this by virtue of its internal relation with the assertion, because it is 'another' assertion and because an assertion is a negation. Within the Third Term the first term is found again, only richer and more determinate, together with the second term, whose determination has been added to the first determination. The Third Term turns back to the first term by negating the second one, by negating therefore the negation and limitation of the first term. It releases the content of the first term, by removing from it that whereby it was incomplete, limited and destined to be negated, or that whereby it was itself negative. Its one-sidedness is thus surmounted and destroyed. To negate this one-sidedness is to negate the negation and posit a higher determination. The contradiction which thrust each term beyond itself, uprooting it from its finitude and inserting it into the total movement, is resolved. The Third Term unites and transcends the contradictories and preserves what was determinate in them. Unity triumphs after a period of fruitful discord. The first term is the immediate one, the second is both mediated and mediator; the Third Term is immediate by virtue of the mediation having been transcended, and simple by virtue of the difference having been transcended.

The transcending is a fundamental determination occurring everywhere ... Whatever is transcended does not thereby become nothing. Nothingness is immediate, whereas a term that has been transcended has been mediated; it is a non-being, but only inasmuch as it is a result arising from a being; it still has within it there-fore the determination from which it arose. This word (*aufheben*) has two meanings; it means to 'keep' or 'preserve' as well as to 'put a stop to' ... [WL I]

The thought of Nothingness is thus simply the still abstract representation of the infinite fertility of the universe. To hypostatize Being or Nothingness, quality or quantity, the cause or the end, is to deny movement. The dialectical reason transcends all the congealed categories of the understanding; it abolishes them inasmuch as they are isolated and thereby re-stores to them their truth within the total movement of reality and of thought, of the content and the form. Quality transcended is quantity; measure (a specific quantum) transcends quantity and unites quality with quantity. Measure transcended is essence or 'Being turned away from its immediacy and its in-different relation with others into a simple unity with itself'. Essence transcended (for it must manifest it-self, being the *Raison d'être*, the principle of deter-minate existence and a totality of determinations and properties, i.e. a 'thing') is the Phenomenon. Once the Phenomenon and the mutual Relation of the deter-minations, properties and parts of the thing are transcended, they become actuality or substantiality, hence causality and reciprocal action. The notion transcends reality or substantiality. The notion transcended becomes objectivity, which is in its turn transcended by the Idea. In transcending itself the Idea emerges from itself and is alienated in Nature; the *aufheben* of Nature is found in the subjective mind, then in the objective mind (morality, art, religion) and finally in absolute Knowledge, that is, the absolute Idea, the identity of the theoretical Idea and practice, of knowing and productive action. [WL III]

Movement is thus a Transcending. Every reality and every thought must be surmounted in a higher determination which contains them as a content, as an aspect, antecedent or element, that is as a moment in the Hegelian or dialectical sense of that word. Taken in isolation these moments become unthinkable; we can no longer see how they can be distinct when they are linked together, or different when they are united. We cannot see how they are formed or take up their place in the whole. Thought (the understanding) is referred giddily from one term to the other until it immobilizes itself, by an arbitrary decree conducive of error, in a limited position that has been transposed into an absolute, and hence into a fiction or error. The Hegelian dialectic seeks to restore life and movement to the sum of the realities that have been apprehended, to assertions and notions. It involves them in an immense epic of mind. All the contradictions of the world (in which, as soon as thought accepts contradiction instead of excluding it, everything manifests itself as if polarized, contradictory and fluid), all beings therefore and all assertions, together with their relations, interdependencies and interactions, are grasped in the total movement of the content, each one in its own place, at its own 'moment'. The network of facts, forces and concepts becomes Reason. The content, or world, is integrated with the Idea, likewise the whole of history. 'The totality, the sum of the moments of reality, shows itself in its development as necessity.' [E §143]

One-sided determinations – the assertions of the understanding – are not destroyed then by the dialectical Reason. Once it is no longer 'turned against reason' the understanding appears in its true light. Partial truths, finite determinations and limited assertions turn into errors when they claim to be definitive, and attempt to erect themselves above the movement. Understood relatively and reintegrated into the total movement as a moment, every finite determination is true. Every truth is relative, but as a truth it is located in the absolute and has its place within absolute truth. The understanding is a movement within the movement; it asserts, posits, negates and analyses. At a lower level it imitates the activity of creation.

It is essential to note that Hegelian logic does not abolish formal logic but transcends it, that it rescues and preserves it precisely by giving it a concrete significance.

Formal logic is the logic of the instant, of the assertion and the object isolated and protected in their isolation. It is the logic of a simplified world : this table (considered independently of any relation with the activity of creation, and leaving aside the ravages of time) is obviously this table, while this lamp is not that book. Formal logic is the logic of abstraction as such. Language is subject to it, as being a set of symbols which serve to communicate an isolated meaning and which must keep the same meaning during the verbal transmission. But the moment the Becoming or activity have to be expressed, formal logic becomes inadequate. On this point Hegel's demonstration has been borne out by the whole of subsequent philosophy. Formal logic is the logic of common sense. Common sense isolates and immobilizes qualities, properties and aspects of things. Once the Becoming or activity is involved it is hard-pressed and takes refuge in phrases like 'inasmuch as' or 'in this respect', that is 'it accepts responsibility for one thought so as to keep the other one separate and true ... ' [P]

Dialectical logic transcends static assertions but it does not destroy them. It does not reject the principle of identity, it gives it a content.

Being is Being. The universe is one. The force of creation is the same throughout the universe. The Essence, in its manifold manifestations and appearances, is unique. The principle of identity expresses this inner uniqueness of the world and of each being. A stone, inasmuch as it is, is what it is; likewise thought. But the identity we have just expressed is still only abstract, because the stone is not the man who thinks. [E §88] The concrete is an identity both rich and dense, laden with determinations, and containing and maintaining a multiplicity of differences and moments. Unity, so to speak, is perpetually being wrested out of contradiction and Nothingness.

An absolute contradiction would be absolute division, or immediate annihilation. An absolute contradiction in a thing, or between thought and things, would make any immanent activity or thought impossible. Contradiction, like Nothingness, is relative, to an assertion, a degree of Being, or a moment of the development. In Nature it is externality, in life a relation between the individual and the species, etc. For Hegel therefore, there is no question of destroying the principle of identity. Quite the reverse : every contradiction is relative to a certain identity. Conversely, unity is the unity of a contradiction. Without a content, without multiple and contradictory 'moments', unity is void. But contradiction as such is intolerable; the dialectical unity is not a confusion of the contradictory terms as such, but a unity which passes through the contradiction and is re-established at a higher level. The contradiction is a tearing asunder, an internal destruction, an uprooting of Being from itself, a fertilization through Becoming, annihilation and death; but the unity expresses and determines the appearance of the new being, the Third Term. Unity can never expel the relative negation and Nothingness from itself altogether, but to the extent that it fights against contradiction and triumphs, by surmounting the contradictory moments and maintaining them within itself, then a new and higher being is produced. The principle of identity thus becomes concrete and alive.

The unity of contradictories exists only in specific, concrete forms. There are different degrees of contradiction – and unity. A more profound contradiction manifests itself in a more profound demand for unity. Contradiction and unity are historical, they pass through phases. Contradiction is only 'in-itself' in the pure and simple destruction of the existent. In its relation to and its struggle with unity it is determined more concretely as a difference and a differentiation, as a passing of one term into the other and an opposition (a latent contradiction), as an antagonism (a contradiction whose patience is exhausted) and, finally, as an incompatibility (the moment of the resolution and the Transcending). The leaf, the blossom and the fruit form part of the tree and of its development, yet they mark themselves off from it with a certain independence, which even becomes a necessary separation once the fruit is ripe and able to produce another tree.

From the point of view of Hegelian logic, the question: 'Which comes first, contradiction or identity?' has no real meaning. All movement is contradictory because without an immanent contradiction nothing can move. Movement is itself a contradiction, and the contradiction propels the movement. Unity is fluid and a cause of movement. The Becoming therefore is the supreme reality, necessitating an infinite analysis whose first moments are Being and Nothingness, identity and contradiction. What we have here is not Bergson's duration, a Becoming without discontinuity and without drama, an amorphous, abstract and purely psychological movement. Hegel's dialectical movement has a determinate internal structure, a structure which is itself in motion. It is infinitely rich in determinations and contains an infinity of moments. The Becoming is a whole, which the dialectical Reason grasps in a primary intuition. The analysis breaks up this whole, yet this analysis can be made and is not external to the Becoming; it is a movement within the movement, which it only breaks up irrevocably if it believes itself to be complete and posits absolute assertions. It determines 'moments' within the movement which are ideal, that is abstract, but which nevertheless have a relative reality and, inasmuch as they are transcended, return into the composition of actuality. Each moment can be analysed in its turn. As soon as we try to immobilize it, it makes its escape, leaving its 'other' in its place, a contrary moment, which is also real and also transcended. In order to analyse a particular moment it must be taken by surprise in its fluid relationship with its 'other'. Dialectical logic is therefore both a method of analysis and a recreation of the movement of the real, through a movement of thought which is capable of following the creative Becoming in its twists and turns, its accidents and its internal structure.

The normal view of analysis is that it releases, tautologically, a predicate included in the subject; if it is fruitful, as in the sciences, it breaks up this subject and leads to an 'element' whose relation to the whole remains ill-determined. In dialectical logic the element attained by every legitimate analysis is a 'moment' of the whole. The analysis dissects and produces an abstraction, but dialectical logic gives this abstraction a concrete meaning. The synthesis does not exclude the analysis, it includes it. The analysis is dialectical because it leads to contradictory moments. The synthesis is analytical because it restores the unity already implied in the moments.

Formal logic asserts: 'A is A'. Dialectical logic is not saying 'A is not-A', it is not hypostatizing the contradiction or substituting absurdity for formalism. It says:

A is indeed A, but A is also not-A precisely in so far as the proposition 'A is A' is not a tautology but has a real content. A tree is a tree only by being such and such a tree, by bearing leaves, blossom and fruit, by passing through and preserving within itself those moments of its becoming, which analysis can attain but must not isolate ... The blossom, moreover, turns into fruit, and the fruit detach themselves and

41

produce other trees; this expresses a profound relationship, a difference verging on contradiction ...

Formal logic says: 'If a particular proposition is true, it is true'; 'No proposition can be both true and false'; 'Every proposition must be either true or false.' Dialectical logic goes further and asserts: 'If we consider the content, if there is a content, an isolated proposition is neither true nor false; every isolated proposition must be transcended; every proposition with a real content is both true and false, true if it is transcended, false if it is asserted as absolute.' Formal logic limits itself to classifying abstract types of syllogistic inference. Dialectical logic, because it determines the content, has quite different implications. The simpler determinations are found again within the more complex ones. These determinations are obtained by pursuing the analysis of the movement as far as the moment when the content has been reduced to a minimum, and they themselves enter into movement once the reason has related them to each other. They are linked together dialectically and their movement rejoins the total movement. They are therefore laws of movement, guiding principles for the analysis of the more complex and more concrete movements. In every concrete content we have to discover the negation, the internal contradiction, the immanent movement, the positive and the negative. Every determinate existence is, from one point of view, quality (immediate determinability or 'something'), and, from another, extensive or intensive quantity, or degree. Quality and quantity are to be found everywhere, in every domain, degree or sphere of Being and of thought. Every quality or quantity is concrete, and they are therefore joined to each other; every quantity is qualitative, that is a specific measure. However, quantity and quality do not merge, but vary with a certain independence of each other; there can be quantitative changes in the being under consideration without any qualitative destruction. But, at a given moment, the variation in the one reacts on the other; a quantitative change, hitherto continuous, suddenly becomes qualitative. (Hegel takes an example from the Greek philosophers: a head loses its hairs one by one, and at a given moment it is bald.) Quantity, being indifferent in relation to determinability and variable as such, 'is the aspect wherein visible existence is exposed to a sudden assault and destroyed. The concept's cunning lies in grasping a determinate being by the side where its quality does not seem to be involved', [WL I] in such a way that, for example, the growth of a State or a private fortune may bring about its downfall.

Changes in Being are therefore not purely quantitative. There always occurs an 'interruption in the graduality', a sudden and profound change, or discontinuity; water that is growing colder 'all of a sudden becomes hard' at a zero temperature. [WL I] Only in this way can there be 'a coming into being and a passing away', that is a true Becoming. The theory of graduality or pure continuity abolishes the Becoming by assuming that whatever passes away still survives, although imperceptible, and that whatever comes into being was already in existence, if only in the form of a tiny seed. In the true Becoming, the just turns into the unjust and excessive virtue into vice. A State which grows quantitatively (in population or wealth) changes its nature, its structure and its constitution; it may collapse from within, because of the selfsame constitution which, before it expanded, had made it strong and prosperous.

Movement is therefore a unity of the continuous and the discontinuous, which will have everywhere to be recovered and analysed. There is a 'leap', a discontinuity, a change of qualitative determination or degree, and hence a transcending, whenever a quality has reached its immanent limit, urged on, so to speak, by quantitative changes. In order to understand or predict the qualitative leap we have to study the quantitative changes and determine the point or 'nodal' line where the discontinuity arises.

The Becoming is a continuous development (an evolution) yet at the same time it is punctuated by leaps, by sudden mutations and upheavals. At the same time it is an involution, since it carries with it and takes up again the content from which it began, even while it is forming something new. No Becoming is indefinitely rectilinear.

These 'dialectical laws' are the first analysis and most general expression of the Becoming. One might say that they sum up its essential characteristics, without which there cannot be a Becoming, but only stagnation or, more precisely, a 'stubborn' repetition by the understanding of an abstract element. These very general determinations of the Becoming prove themselves to be necessary by issuing from each other and linking themselves together into a Becoming. The fact that there are three ('if one wants to count them,' says Hegel) of these dialectical determinations is still only a superficial and external aspect of our mode of cognition. In itself the movement is one.

In this Becoming of thought, by linking the categories together, the Hegelian mind 'descends into itself', grasping and absorbing its content. It grasps it by overcoming everything which separates or disperses, by destroying the negative element as such, and by negating the negation. Mind defines itself as the highest unity, possessing manifold aspects. As an immanent activity and Becoming it possesses its own movement within itself. It can posit, pass over and transcend, and then recapitulate these successive stages rationally. It produces its own movement by the negation of every partial moment, but this movement does not mean that it escapes from itself. Mind is a whole, it is the total movement.

The Identity which is completely full and concrete, and contains all the determinations, is the Idea. In the dialectical movement it becomes 'for-itself' what it had been 'in-itself', i.e. virtually, moments that could be isolated and externalized, determinations that had had to be posited in themselves and hence negatively, so that they could then be negated and brought back into the true infinite of the Idea. The Idea is recovered in the content, which it has deployed so as to manifest itself, and so as to make the content explicit and concentrate it in itself. Mind and the Idea or, to be more exact, absolute Knowledge, are the supreme Third Term which contains and resolves the oppositions and contradictions of the universe. The Idea negates itself by manifesting or 'alienating' itself, but it negates itself in conformity with its own nature, it remains itself in its alienation, then recovers this nature in a multiform process.

45

Law, art and religion are so many distinct domains, so many avenues by which Mind, by absorbing into itself an ever higher content, comes to the possession of itself, to the Idea. Phenomenal Mind, related to an existing object, is consciousness. 'The science of Consciousness is called the Phenomenology of Mind.' Phenomenology is a higher psychology, which deals with 'Mind forming itself and educating itself in its concept', its manifestations being 'moments of its giving birth to itself through itself'. The history of philosophy and the philosophy of history retrace the external existence of Mind, and its successive stages. Logic, finally, is at once the richest and the poorest of philosophical and scientific studies. It cements the stonework of the Hegelian edifice solidly together. It is a 'science of thought', thought being itself the determinability of the content, 'the universal element in every content'. Although it works with abstractions dialectical logic is within Truth, it is itself Truth. The logical movement of the concept can be found again – specifically – in every domain or degree.

A critique of Hegel's dialectic

Hegel's ambition coincides with that of philosophy, with the most secret desire of the life of the mind, seen as expansion and dominion : to exclude nothing, to leave nothing outside itself, to abandon and transcend every one-sided position. It is linked with that fundamental appetite for Being which must be maintained, cleansed if possible from magic, i.e. from illusion.

Hegelianism asserts implicitly that all conflicts can be resolved, without mutilation or renunciation, in an expansion of Being; it asserts that in the life of Mind there is no need for options, alternatives or sacrifices. Innumerable conflicts are objectively experienced, but none of them lasts for ever. Every contradiction can be transcended in a forward leap of Mind. Hegelianism remains therefore the only road a spiritual optimism or dynamism can take if it is to be formulated.

Just as much as a doctrine and a logical method, Hegelianism represents a type of spiritual life that is still valid. Not to aim at acquiescing too hastily to ourselves or to the world; not to hide from ourselves the contradictions in the world, in man and in each individual, but, on the contrary, to accentuate them, however much we may suffer, because it is fruitful to be torn asunder and because, once the contradictions have become unbearable, the need to transcend them becomes stronger than any resistance on the part of the elements that are passing away; such is the principle of a spiritual life both sorrowful and joyous, wholly rational and unconfused. It says 'Yes' to the world, but not just 'yes' in some blind ecstasy, it also says 'No' and rejects what reveals itself to be sterile or moribund.

Hegel knew that the conflict and division within modern man are not an invention of the philosophers. As he shows at the beginning of his *Aesthetic*, modern culture forces man to live 'in two worlds which contradict one another. On the one hand we see man living in the ordinary, temporal actuality of this world, weighed down by want and wretchedness, in thrall to matter; on the other hand he can raise himself up to Ideas, to a kingdom of thought and of freedom; inasmuch as he is Will he gives himself

47

laws.' But even as he does so 'he strips the world of its living actuality and resolves it into abstractions.' Thus flesh and spirit, everyday reality and thought, real necessity and ideal freedom, actual servitude and the theoretical power of the intelligence, the wretchedness of concrete existence and the splendid but fictive sovereignty of the Idea, all are in conflict. For the past hundred years this unhappy cleavage of the modern consciousness has done nothing but grow more acute, until it is now intolerable.

Yet did Hegel really grasp the entire content of human experience? Did he grasp it in its authentic movement? Did he really set out from the content and extract the form from it without falsifying it? Did he really raise all the degrees and profundity of the content to thought, without subordinating it to a preconceived form and without turning back to the content as immediately given?

In the first place, Hegelianism, being a system, involves one essential presupposition – whereas it claims not to admit any presuppositions at all. Is it conceivable that the limited mind of an individual, of a philosopher, should be able to grasp the entire content of human experience? If this content is, as Hegel says it is, infinitely rich – such a richness or superabundance being alone worthy of Mind – his claim can no longer be upheld. The content will be attained only through the joint efforts of many thinking individuals, in a progressive expansion of consciousness. Hegel's own claim encloses and limits the content and makes it unworthy of Mind.

To enclose the content of art within a series of aesthetic definitions reduces it to an abstract form. In point of fact, in every great work of art, each age and each individual grasps a new content, a new aspect of it which surprises us; only thus can the work of art be a unity of the finite and the infinite, an infinite both determinate and alive. The content develops, it becomes richer and more profound. Mind's life of discovery and creation did not come to an end with Hegel. With Nietzsche, for example, Greek art appeared in a new perspective. We have continued to explore Nature, life and human beings; fresh conflicts have appeared, fresh contents and fresh problems which cannot be solved in advance. Other topics, other social and spiritual groups are asking to be raised to the level of the spiritual life and of the Idea, to be uprooted, in principle and in practice, from immediacy and necessity. Does not Nature, which is life as given to us, spontaneously, provide us with a content in itself infinitely rich? Hegel's speculative attitude is in a particularly awkward position vis-à-vis this content; it seeks to exhaust and define it, and introduce it into absolute Knowledge, that is into the Hegelian metaphysic. For him the starry heavens are no more marvellous than an eruption of the skin. Error and evil are to be preferred to the regular trajectories of the heavenly bodies or the innocence of plants because error and evil are evidence of the existence of Mind. In relation to the Idea, the luxuriance of Nature, its ambivalence, its vitality, its fantasy and its incessant generation of new and aberrant types, are merely a form of impotence: 'Nature is abstract and does not attain to true existence.'

If Hegelianism had been able to attain and define the entire content, what would have been left for autonomous art and science, for future ages and for action? Inasmuch as it is a finished system, Hegelianism leads, like traditional formalism, to a sharp conflict between invention and knowledge, between fruitfulness and rigour.

Action has specific laws, whether it be a relapse from contemplation and the inner life or, which is more likely, a fertilization of the mind through contact with the outside world or, alternatively, a distinct essence, parallel with thought and juxtaposed with other essences, their unity being transcendent. Whatever the case, action is a reality! It forms part of that given existence from which the 'magical' mind which claims to grasp and arrest the world may well emerge in order to hurl itself into the void but which it can transcend only illusorily. Action is a reality. The understanding says: 'In order to take to the water we must first know how to swim.' Action resolves vicious circles, or the contradictions of static thought. Practice is creative, it cannot be deduced from the concept. It has its own exigencies, its own discipline – its own logic perhaps. Since Hegel's time the problem of action and practice has imposed itself on philosophy, which has attempted to define the specific categories of action, and has sometimes even turned action against thought, by striving to conceive of a pure action, action which is nothing but action; in this way it has applied the understanding and formalism to the new problem of action.

True, Hegel did give action a part to play; he saw the absolute Idea as a unity of practice and knowledge, of the creative activity and thought. Mind transcends the immediate; it modifies the object, transforming and assimilating it. Action imitates the mind, whenever one eats an item of food for example. Hegel's Mind feeds off the world and devours it, causing it to disappear. But Hegel did not elucidate action in itself, inasmuch as it comes up against an object which it cannot cause to disappear more or less 'spiritually'. Hegel did not develop Kant's analysis of the specifically practical Reason. He determined a concept of action, and confused action with the thought of action. But if action has its own laws and content how is its domain to be limited? Action proclaims itself: '*Am Anfang war die Tat.*' Rational thought, then, has got to be rescued, just as Hegel tried to rescue logic, by transcending it.

Hegel was not content merely to deepen the content and make it explicit in order to attain the form, he reduced it to thought, by claiming to grasp it 'totally' and exhaust it. He insists on the rigorously and definitively determinate form which the content acquires in Hegelianism. All the determinations must be linked together in order to become intelligible. As far as Hegel is concerned, these connections are not discovered gradually, or obtained by an experimental method; they are fixed. The sum of them, the totality, forms a circle. 'Philosophy forms a circle. Whatever philosophy begins with is immediately relative and must appear as a result from a different terminal point.' [PR] Any other philosophy is simply a subjective feeling and contingent in relation to the content. Only a perfect systemization can guarantee the possession of the entire content and turn philosophy into a science.

Truth ceases to be thought of as the unity of the form and the content, but is defined by the agreement of the form with itself, by its internal coherence, by the formal identity of thought. And spiritual freedom is not defined as a taking possession of the content through a 'becoming aware', but is determined as a setting-free of Mind in relation to the content as such – experience, life or action – by means of the notion and the idea.

The form therefore is not criticized in terms of the content or derived from making the latter explicit. It is posited in terms of the exigencies of formal rigour and the necessities of philosophical systemization. Having asserted the primacy of the content, Hegel declares that 'logical thoughts are not moments exclusive in relation to those thoughts, because they are the absolute foundation of all things.' [E §XIV] Thought is thus the secret source of the content. It is only an illusion that Mind receives its content from outside, in accordance with the unphilosophical presuppositions of observation and experience. Nature appears to be the presupposition of Mind only up until that moment when the supreme truth, the Idea, is determined. Nature disappears into this truth. The movement of thought is only a turning back on itself. 'The internal birth or becoming of substance is a passing over into the external; inversely, the Becoming of determinate Being is the internal essence taking hold of itself once again.' The content allows itself to be shut up in this enclosed, circular system only because it was itself the emanation of the Mind that posited this form. 'The whole may be compared to a circle containing other circles ... in such a way that the system of these particular elements forms the totality of the Idea.' [E §XV] It is no longer a matter of raising the content freely to the notion, but of finding in the content a certain form of the notion, posited *a priori* in relation to the content : circular, enclosed and total in a special sense of that word, to wit as a closed totality. Thought grasps only itself. All the thinking subject does is to witness this development of the Idea. The interesting thing for the other sciences is to recover the forms of logic. [E §XIV] And science 'contains thought inasmuch as thought is the thing itself, or in other words the thing in itself, inasmuch as it is pure thought.' The subject-matter of cognition, or content, is thus determined by the form.

More generally, Hegel's dialectical logic can be interpreted in several ways, or rather two or even three different movements of thought can be found in it:

(*a*) The dialectic is seen as an analysis of the movement. The method assumes the content; it breaks up the unity of the Becoming only to recover it again later. Ultimately, after an infinite analysis, the movement of thought coincides with the spontaneous movement of the world and the content.

(*b*) Instead of expressing and reflecting the movement of the content, the dialectic produces this movement. It is not so much a method of analysis as a method of synthetic and systematic construction of the content.

(*c*) The dialectic is seen as resulting from the alienation of the Idea. At the point where it starts is to be found the potentiality of the Idea which emerges from itself, divides, becomes 'other' and produces the dialectic.

Each of these interpretations can be supported from what Hegel wrote, but it would seem that the second one is the most authentically Hegelian. The *Phenomenology* itself, which lays so much stress on the content of consciousness, and on alienation and the externalization of Mind in the world of things, states that: 'The content, defined more precisely ... is Mind, which reviews itself and reviews itself inasmuch as it is Mind.' And the final chapter of the *Greater Logic* comes to the conclusion that the method is the absolute, unique, supreme and infinite force, which no object will be able to resist. The method is at once 'soul and substance'; or, more clearly still: 'The logical Idea is its own content inasmuch as it is an infinite form.' The absolute Idea, released for itself, 'has been made manifest by the fact that, in it, the determination no longer takes the form of a content but simply of a form.' It transcends its positing as a content. In the absolute Idea, logic recovers the simple unity of the starting-point: by virtue of the mediation and of the transcending of this mediation, immediate Being has become an Idea which has achieved identity with itself. 'The method is the pure concept related only to itself; it is therefore that simple relation to self which is Being.' The concept no longer appears as external to the content, which it had been in subjective reflection. In absolute Knowledge the concept has become its own content. The absolute Idea becomes a beginning for other spheres and other sciences: those of Nature and history. Absolute Knowledge therefore, instead of being the final term and 'end' of thought, can be taken as a starting-point. Starting from the Idea we can reconstruct the world.

It is not certain whether these three interpretations or dialectical movements are compatible. The theory of alienation becomes oddly blurred in the *Greater Logic*. Hegel wants to show that the Idea, positing itself as a unity of the concept and reality, 'is absorbed into the immediacy of Being', becomes Nature, although it does not cease to be itself, simple, transparent and free. 'The transition must be understood in this sense, that the Idea lets go of itself freely (*sich selbst entlässt*), absolutely sure of itself and resting in itself.' Thus the Idea is nothing more than infinite rest. And as it says in the last paragraph of the *Lesser Logic* (which elsewhere lays so much stress on the content), the Idea 'resolves to deliver itself freely of the moment of its particularity, of the first determination of the other being'. It is rather curious to compare these passages with those, especially in the *Phenomenology* (or even in the *Logics*), which express the profound and disruptive activity of infinite negativity, subjectivity, freedom and the Transcending. 'In so far as it is a subject, the living substance is pure and simple negativity, a process which divides the simple, duplicates the terms and sets them in opposition to each other,' says the *Phenomenology*.

Hegel does not prove that this calm externalization of the Idea releases contradictory existences and not juxtaposed existences or essences, quite simply external one to another. On the contrary, he accepts religion, law and art to be distinct domains, contradictory neither amongst themselves nor with philosophy, and hence simply juxtaposed. Religion and philosophy have a common content and this content is subtracted from the development, from succession in time. [GP,E §XX] By believing that it can grasp the whole content Hegelianism limits the content it can accept, accepts this uncritically and finally subtracts it from the dialectical Becoming. In which case the dialectical contradiction exists only for and through the finite, individual mind.

Sometimes Hegel posits absolute, motionless Being, eternal self-knowledge, an objective identity which abolishes all contradiction for ever. The philosopher participates in this absolute Knowledge and extracts the entire world from out of his head; the form of identity gives birth to the content. This system is built up like a piece of rigid architecture, made up of superimposed triangles suspended by their apices. Then, perhaps, Hegel feels Being starting to shudder and elude him, so he posits a substance even stranger and more alien than Being – Negativity. The positive or determination is itself a negation and a participation (*Mitteilung*) in the negativity, which is the 'soul', the 'turning-point in the movement of the concept', the 'mighty power' of thought, which destroys and transcends. Negativity which, inasmuch as it is an infinite power identical with itself, is a hypostatized negation, thus acquires a transcendent existence; it is an absolute Nothingness of which the positive is no more than a momentary manifestation instantly suppressed. It is an active Nothingness, a mystical and omnipresent abyss, from which all the forces of life and matter tumble like mysterious cataracts before falling back into it again. Negativity is infinite and cruel, and Hegelianism becomes a subjective mysticism. It might be thought of as something constructed by the internal tempo of Mind, moving within the eternal present, or else, as Heidegger puts it, as an attempt at the analysis of the 'ontological structure' of death. The objective content vanishes.

Hegelian speculation is still steeped in 'magical' ideas. By positing a magical participation in absolute

Being (conceived of as knowledge and reason), it combines the magical schema with an attempt to be more fully rational. At the same time it is a first metaphysic of Nothingness. It oscillates between absolute Object and absolute Subject, between Being and Nothingness, between Knowledge and a magical mysticism.

Hegel's system, inasmuch as it is a system, abolishes both contradiction and the Becoming. Contradiction is reduced to a logical essence, a relation determinable *a priori* which the mind automatically meets with in every single thing; it is only an approximation to the truth, relative to the positions adopted by our finite understanding. Being no longer attached to the spontaneous, given movement of thought's content, it loses its objectivity. What we have is no longer the concrete unity of specific contradictions, but an absolute identity – Being or Nothingness – posited in advance, for all eternity.

But contradiction does not allow itself to be destroyed by Hegel any more than by the pure logicians; it takes an ironic revenge on him. Hegelianism sought to put an end to the Becoming by seeing it as a Becoming and enclosing it quietly in a circle. But it is an illusion to see the Becoming as a quiet circle, as a resting-place for thought within itself, or as a fulfilment of Mind. Hegel wanted to resolve and transcend all the contradictions of the world, but contradiction and even illogicality remained inside his own system. By making it eternal he immobilizes the reality he claims to be reconstructing, and it is the reality of his own time : with him the metaphysical Third Term takes on the well-

57

known and very unphilosophical features of the Prussian State.

Yet life goes on. States crumble or are transformed. The Hegelian universe therefore is nothing more than the world of the metaphysician Hegel, the creature of his own speculative ambition. It is still not the world of men, in all its dramatic reality. What answer does it hold for the exigencies and the urgent questions of individuals engaged in living, who seek spiritual guidance and earthly salvation? Confronted by Nothingness they hesitate, they would like to fight against death and have an open future before them. Does Hegel keep his promises?

The *Phenomenology* says grandiosely: 'That which seems to take place independently of it (matter) and to be an activity directed against it, is its own activity.' An unwise promise! The world is only justified if it is 'my' handiwork, I mean the creation of whatever is most validly human and spiritual in me. Hegel pledges himself to proving to me, a man-in-the-world, that even that which causes me suffering is the product of the human and spiritual activity in me. He pledges himself to justify the past, the present and the problems of the present, as the preconditions for the existence and formation of my freedom. Now, I do not recognize myself in the fictive drama of the Idea which 'lets itself go' in the creation of the world, is alienated and then recovers itself in the Hegelian system. Hegelianism is a dogma, it demands a self-discipline, a renunciation of individual experience and the problems of individual existence. When the *Phenomenology* describes the torment of unrealized being, I find it moving; but the cosmic adventures of Mind are independent of us. Hegelianism does not have magic powers, it cannot efface or justify what causes us actual suffering or hinders us from living.

We come up against hostile forces, alien beings and tyrannies. Is it simply an attitude of Mind which makes these forces of destiny so oppressive and relentless? In order to be delivered from hostility and oppression or to give our consent to them, is it enough simply to become aware of them 'as such'? Hegelianism does not provide a solution. Inasmuch as it is a system and a dogma it reproduces within Mind the limited relation between Master and Slave. It is nothing more than a finite object.

Yet Hegel's ambition remains valid and coincides with that of philosophy. A way has been opened. Perhaps it is possible to transcend Hegelianism on its own terms, from inside, by starting from its own contradictions and preserving what is essential in its mode of operation. Perhaps we must accept the 'rich content' of life in all its immensity: Nature, spontaneity, action, widely differing cultures, fresh problems. It may swamp our minds, we may have to explore it and study it in greater depth without being able to exhaust it, but we must open our minds to it. The form to which thought raises the content must be seen as fluid and capable of improvement. Thought must accept the contradictions and conflicts in the content, it must determine their transcending and their solutions in accordance with the movement of that content, and not impose *a priori* and systematic forms on it. Little by little the Becoming will be re-possessed through and through, in all its prodigious wealth of moments, aspects and elements. A transcended Hegelianism will integrate and elaborate dialectical logic in conformity with the nature of the dialectical movement itself, of the Becoming taken authentically as absolute experience.

Historical materialism

This critical examination of Hegelianism matches, in its broad outlines and its conclusions, the one which Marx (in collaboration with Engels) undertook between 1843 and 1859, and which led him to dialectical materialism. Their lengthy inquiry into philosophy, science and politics led Marx and Engels from jurisprudence to economics, from liberalism to socialism, and from Hegelian idealism to a highly developed form of materialism.

From 1844 onwards, for practical reasons and because the Prussian State seemed to him to be oppressive for actual living men, Marx ceased to look on the State as 'the actuality of the ethical idea'. [PR §257] Religion and philosophy cannot have the same content, because philosophy must first of all criticize that solid pillar of institutions: established religion. 'Every critique must be preceded by a critique of religion.' [N] Marx was later to write that from this time onwards he had realized 'that juridical relations, like forms of government, cannot be explained either in themselves or by the supposed evolution of the human Mind, but that they have their roots in the conditions of material existence which Hegel ... embraces as a whole under the name of civil society ... ' From now on, therefore, Marx will develop the content of Hegelianism (the concrete theory of civil society, of the 'system of needs' and of social relations) against Hegel's fixed system and its political consequences.

The *Economico-Philosophical Manuscript*, which Marx wrote in 1844, sees as essential the question: 'Where does Hegelian logic get us?' The *Manuscript*'s answer is a remarkable formula: 'Logic is the money of Mind.' Logic is only a part of the content, its most elaborate, impersonal and malleable aspect, and the one which has been most fully fashioned by intellectual exchange. Within the logical categories there remain a few traces of the content and its movement, and abstract though these may be we can still reconstitute the movement and recover the content. But logic is only a human value, expressed in abstract thought, its essence having become indifferent and unreal. It forms part therefore of the 'alienation' of living men because, like Nature, it disregards both him and concrete existence. How can the world be deduced from it? And how can it be the essence of human thought?

The theoretical and philosophical origins of dialectical materialism are to be found not in Hegel's *Logics* but in his *Phenomenology*. For Marx this was the key to the Hegelian system. It is here that we recover the actual content of human life, that upward movement 'from earth to heaven'. It therefore contains the positive aspect of Hegel's idealism. Hegel resolves the world into ideas but he is not content merely to record passively the objects of thought, he seeks to expose the act of their production. [I,I] The result is that, 'within the speculative exposition', he gives us a real exposition which grasps the thing itself. [HF] Here, according to the *Manuscript* of 1844, Hegel considers 'the creation of man by himself as a process ... ' He examines the objectification of man in a world of external objects and his de-objectification (his becoming aware of himself) as a transcending of his alienation. He half sees that labour is essentially a creative activity and grasps that objective man – the only real man – is the result of this creative power. According to the *Phenomenology* the relation of man to himself and to the human species, his realization of himself, is made possible only by the activity of the whole of humanity, and presupposes the entire history of the human race.

Unfortunately, the *Phenomenology* does not properly understand man's alienation. Hegel sees an alienation in what man realizes, the world of objective products or things created by man. In the human powers and objects that have acquired an external form : wealth, the State, religion, which uproot man from himself by subordinating him to his own products, Hegel sees a realization of Mind. In fact, Hegel 'replaces man by consciousness'. He replaces the whole of human reality by the Consciousness which knows itself. 'Hegel turns man into the man of consciousness, instead of turning consciousness into the consciousness of real men, living in the real world.' Now, this consciousness is nothing more than Mind, metaphysically dissociated from Nature, which is itself separated from man and disguised as a purely external existence. Mind (absolute Knowledge or absolute Subject-Object) is the unity of these terms, abstract man in a Nature metaphysically transposed. 'When Hegel studies wealth, or the power of the State, as essences which have become alien to human nature, he takes them only in their abstract form; they are beings of reason, alienations of pure thought ... This is why the whole history of alienation and its inverse movement are nothing more than the history of the production of abstract thought, of speculative, logical thought ... '

Quite rightly Hegel lays stress on the split within man, and on his real conflicts. But 'what passes in Hegel as characterizing the essence of this split which must be abolished, is not the fact that the human essence is objectified inhumanly, but that it is objectified by being distinguished from abstract thought'. Hegel always has in mind the abstract act of positing something, of positing a logical assertion. He defines this act as giving a series of abstract products and then withdrawing from them. He poses the problem of the 'appropriation of the essential forces of man which have become objects, and alien objects', but this appropriation takes place only in man's consciousness of himself, in abstraction. 'In Hegel the claiming of the objective world on behalf of man, the knowledge of the fact that ... religion, wealth, etc., are nothing more than the alienated reality of man – the road therefore to a truly human reality – (take on) a form such that sensibility, religion and the authority of the State appear as spiritual essences.' All that we find in the *Phenomenology* therefore, is a 'disguised' and mystified critical analysis of these essences and moments of the mind. In actual fact, it is natural that a living, natural being should possess the objects of his desires and of his being. These objects are not his alienation. On the contrary, he is 'alienated' by not possessing them; he is alienated by being temporarily dominated by a world that is 'other' even though he himself gave birth to it, and so equally real. In this alienation man remains an actual, living being who must overcome his alienation through 'objective action'. The critique of the *Phenomenology* therefore, and of Hegel's theory of alienation, opens the way for a positive humanism, which has to transcend and unite idealism and naturalism (or materialism).

The *Manuscript* also asserts that the dialectic in Hegel between Being and Nothingness is suspect. Cognition establishes the nothingness of the object, which is precisely what unites the dialectical theory and the theory of alienation. The object is identical with the act of knowing: it is its alienation. The object is a mirage, a false appearance of cognition, which opposes itself and hence opposes Nothingness to itself. As a relation with the object, cognition is outside itself, although it remains itself; it has been 'alienated'. The positive theory of man's alienation can but reject this dialectic between Being and Nothingness.

In Hegel thought purports to be the whole of life. By passing through and transcending his 'other' being, man claims to recover himself again in pure Mind. Thought recovers itself in madness, inasmuch as it is madness! The 'alienated' life is recognized as the true life, in religion, in the law, in political life and, finally, in philosophy. 'To know and to live is to posit oneself, to assert oneself in contradiction to oneself, in contradiction to the knowledge and essence of the object.' The Hegelian negation of negation is not therefore the assertion of man's true essence by the negation of his imaginary essence. On the contrary, it abolishes the concrete essence and transforms into a subject the false objectivity or abstraction: pure thought or 'absolute' knowledge without an object.

In the Hegelian Transcending, the determinations that have been transcended remain as immobile moments of the total movement: law and private property, the State, religion etc. 'Their fluid essence manifests itself only philosophically.' A simple thought can be overcome by a pure thought. Phenomenology 'allows the material and sensible substratum of the different alienated forms of consciousness to survive'; it describes the relation between Master and Slave, but actual slavery remains and Hegel's freedom is purely mental. It describes the divided mind and expresses the spiritual malaise of the modern world but seeks to put an end to them only in and through philosophy. Every being, every man, thus acquires a second existence, philosophical existence, which, for Hegel, is the only real and authentic one. Man exists philosophically; his religious or his political existence are, in actual fact, religio-philosophical, politico-philosophical etc. Thus he is religious only in so far as he is a philosopher of religion. Hegel denies real religiousness only to immediately assert and re-establish it as an 'allegory of philosophical existence'. Consequently 'this ideal transcending leaves its object intact in reality'. Hegel opposes non-philosophical immediacy, then accepts its immediate reality philosophically.

The *Economico-Philosophical Manuscript* rejects dialectical logic only to accept the theory of alienation, by modifying it profoundly. This position became clearer during the years 1845–6, when Marx and Engels were judging the philosophy of Feuerbach against the humanism to which they had been led by their own experience and by their critique of Hegelianism. Examination of the evolution of Marx's

E

thought does not reveal a 'Feuerbach phase' but rather an integration and, at the same time, a continuing critique of Feuerbach's ideas.

The young left-wing Hegelians who were seeking to go beyond Hegel depended on him too directly to be able to undertake an 'extended critique' of Hegelianism, from which they had borrowed fragments: isolated categories, such as the consciousness of self, for example. [DI] These young Hegelians made a pseudo-critique of religion; they wanted to give up theology while still remaining theologians, [DI] and merely changed the names of things and of categories, replacing Hegel's 'substance' or 'subjectivity' with 'Man in general', 'the Unique' or 'Consciousness'. They took a religious view of these categories, and instead of analysing the representations of religion, 'canonized' the world as given. Consequently all they set out to change was consciousness, by interpreting the existing world differently and thus accepting it by virtue of this fresh interpretation.

'Compared with Hegel, Feuerbach has little to offer', Marx was to write in 1865, 'yet he marked an epoch.'[1] Indeed, according to Marx and Engels, Feuerbach was the only one of the young Hegelians to have achieved anything of consequence. To the speculative raptures of Hegel he opposed a 'sober philosophy', by laying down 'the broad principles for any critique of Hegelian speculation and consequently of all metaphysics'. [HF II] Feuerbach's philosophy annihilated the dialectic of the concept, 'that war of the gods which the philosophers alone can know'. Into the foreground Feuerbach put man. He criticized Hegel, moreover, as a Hegelian. Hegel is contradict-

[1] In an article on Proudhon in the *Sozial-demokrat*.

ory: if mind becomes Nature and matter, then matter becomes mind. [HF II][1] Reality and truth must be restored to Nature by using Hegel's own methods.

Feuerbach's great 'feat', Marx had already declared in the 1844 *Manuscript*, was to have: (1) proved that philosophy is only religion, logically systematized. It must be condemned, like religion, as being a form of human alienation. Hegel starts from alienation, denies it through philosophy, then re-establishes it within the speculative Idea. Speculation itself must be transcended; (2) founded true materialism by making man's relation to man the fundamental principle of any theory; (3) opposed to Hegel's negation of negation, which declares itself to be the absolute positive, the positive based positively on itself: Nature, the living man, material subject and object.

But his doctrine is still a restricted one. He reduces man to the isolated, biological and passive individual, and hence still to an abstraction. Feuerbach's 'man' is still only the individual member of the bourgeoisie, and a typically German one at that. [DI] Feuerbach leaves out of account what in man is activity, community, co-operation, or relation between the individual and the human species, that is practical, historical and social man. He ignores therefore actual concrete man, for 'the human being, man's being, is a complex of social relations'. [DI]

Feuerbach's humanism is therefore based on a myth: pure Nature. Nature and the object seem to him to have been 'given for all eternity', in a mysterious harmony with man which the philosopher alone

[1] See also Feuerbach: *Grundsätze der Philosophie der Zukunft*.

can perceive. The object is posited as an object of intuition, not as a product of the activity of society or praxis. Feuerbach's Nature is that of the virgin forest or of an atoll recently arisen in the Pacific Ocean. His materialism is therefore, in one essential aspect, inferior to Hegel's idealism: the latter had started from man's activity and, actually, if one-sidedly, had attempted to elucidate and elaborate this activity. Hegel saw that man is not given biologically, but produces himself in history, through life in society, that he creates himself in a process. [M 1844]

Feuerbach's materialism remains one-sided and contradictory. For him, human activity, in so far as he examines it, is theoretical and abstract. Man is seen as a material object, not as sensible activity, and his sensibility does not appear as a productive potentiality. Feuerbach therefore has not broken away from that scholastic philosophy which poses the question of the existence of things and the value of thought independently of practice. [DI] In such a materialism, inspired by that of the eighteenth century, the thought, needs and ideas of individuals are explained by education, but this explains nothing, because the educators themselves need to have been educated. [DI]

Feuerbach shows that religion is an alienation of the secular or profane world. But how has it come about that this profane world should have been thus duplicated and projected into the clouds? It must itself be divided, split and unconscious of itself. Feuerbach does not explain alienation historically, by starting from the life of the human species. For him religious feeling is simply a sort of fixed and fatal error of the isolated individual, cut off from the species. He does not see it as the product of a particular social situation. His humanism is therefore restricted to the contemplation of isolated individuals in contemporary society. Now, this society is itself only a form of the alienation that has got to be transcended. The world must be transformed, not merely interpreted anew.

It is true that Feuerbach puts himself forward as a 'community man', but what practical significance can this formula have? [DI] He seeks to show that men always have need of one another, therefore all he wants to produce is a 'proper awareness of an existing fact'. All he sees in the human are spontaneous and affective relationships, he never grasps the social world 'as the total, living activity of the individuals who comprise it'. [DI] Feuerbach idealizes love and friendship, as if they were improved by being religious! He locates them outside the real, within the ideal and the future. He cannot rise above an abstract conception of man, of human alienation or of the transcending of this alienation.

And yet 'from the fact that Feuerbach showed the world of religion to be an illusory projection of the earthly world, a question was posed for German philosophy which he himself did not resolve: how do men get such illusions into their heads? Even for the German theorists this question opened the way for a materialist conception of the world'. [DI] Instead of seeking to understand or construct Being and beings without presuppositions, this conception observes 'the material presuppositions as such'. For this reason it is truly critical.

In point of fact, real individuals, their actions and

their conditions of existence, both those that they are given and those they create, can be observed empirically. The mode of production of life is a mode of life of individuals. Individuals are according to how they produce their life. 'Consciousness does not determine life, life determines consciousness.' [DI] We must start from man as both actual and active and from the actual process of living (which is continued and reproduced every day) and represent the ideological reflections and echoes of this process.

If man is to attain to consciousness, at least four pre-conditions or presuppositions are necessary : (a) production of the means of subsistence; (b) the production of fresh needs, the first one having been satisfied and its instrument acquired; this constitutes the 'first historical fact' and separates man from animality; (c) the organization of reproduction, that is of the family; (d) the co-operation of individuals and the practical organization of social labour. [DI] Consciousness is therefore, right from the start, a product of society, and it remains so. To start with, consciousness was simply animal and biological, a 'herd-consciousness'. Subsequently it has become real and effective, especially with the division of labour. However, the moment there is a division of labour into material and spiritual, the moment consciousness exists for itself, it is able to imagine itself as being something other than the consciousness of the existing praxis. It loses sight of its own pre-conditions. The new-born reflection of the conscious individual breaks up the social totality at the precise moment when this totality is developing and expanding but also when, with the division of labour, any activity is no longer anything more than a fragmentary one. Thus do ideological fantasies become possible. Moreover, the division of labour assigns production and consumption to different individuals. 'Division of labour and property are identical expressions.' The community comes into conflict with individuals. In the end 'the power proper to man becomes an alien power which opposes and subjugates him instead of being controlled by him'. Each man is confined to his own sphere, he is the prisoner of his own activity, subjected to a totality he can no longer comprehend. 'This reification of social activity and of our product into a power which escapes from our control, which disappoints our expectations and reduces our calculations to dust, is one of the principal moments of historical development.' This is the actual alienation of actual men, whose most notable forms are slavery, the class war and the State. The State is an 'illusory community', but based on existing connections: it intervenes in the class-war as a referee, by claiming to represent the general interest, whereas it really represents the interests of the social group which wields the political power.

This alienation of man can be transcended, but only under practical conditions. It must have grown 'intolerable' by confronting 'the masses deprived of property with an existing world of wealth and culture'; and this assumes a high degree of development of human potentialities. Otherwise the abolition of alienation could only universalize privation, instead of wealth, abundance and power.

The *German Ideology*, therefore, indicates the fundamental theses of historical materialism. Set in motion by the philosophical investigation of the problem of alienation and led on by a desire to make humanism more profound and more concrete, historical materialism integrates and transcends the philosophy of Feuerbach. It takes as its starting-point the most philosophical of Hegel's theories: the theory of alienation. It integrates this theory by profoundly transforming it. The creation of man by himself is a process; the human passes through and transcends moments that are inhuman, historical phases that are the 'other' of the human. But it is practical man who creates himself in this way. By transposing it, Hegel had expressed the essence of the historical process. Feuerbach had indicated the real subject of this process, but, oddly enough, only by reducing the scope and extent of Hegel's theory. Historical materialism, clearly expressed in the *German Ideology*, achieves that unity of idealism and materialism foreshadowed and foretold in the 1844 *Manuscript*.

Once it has been formulated, historical materialism turns against the philosophy from which it had issued, against Hegelianism, against Feuerbach, against philosophy in general. The philosophical attitude is contemplative. Such an attitude is a mutilated and one-sided one, and a distant consequence of the division of labour. Now, philosophy comes precisely to this conclusion, that the truth is to be found in totality. Thereby it condemns itself, since philosophy cannot be the supreme, effectual, total activity. The true is the concrete; philosophical abstractions have hardly any actual effect. There is no immobile absolute, no spiritual 'beyond'. The propositions of the *perennis philosophia* are either tautologies or else acquire a definite meaning only through some historical or empirical content. 'To raise oneself above the world through pure reflection is, in reality, to remain imprisoned in reflection.' [DI] True, concrete universality is based on the praxis. Materialism seeks to give thought back its active force, the one which it had before consciousness became separated from work, when it was still linked directly with practice. The act which posited human thought and made man separate from the animals, and from Nature was a fully creative act, even though it has led to a split within the human reality. The total power of creation must be recovered, at a higher level. Historical materialism fulfils philosophy by transcending it. It takes the – supremely philosophical – decision not to be misled by the illusions of successive epochs and to create a truly universal doctrine. The three requirements of philosophy – efficacy, truth and the universality of its ideas – cannot be met on the philosophical plane. Speculation must be transcended. 'Independent philosophy loses the medium of its existence (*Existenzmedium*) whenever we imagine reality. In its place can come only a summary of the most general results of the study of the historical development.' [DI] 'We must ignore philosophy and set ourselves as ordinary men to the study of the real, for which there exists an immense subject-matter that the philosophers naturally know nothing of.' Philosophies were 'ideologies', that is transpositions of the real, ineffectual and one-sided theories, unaware of their own pre-conditions and content, always putting particular interests forward as universal ones by the use of 'reified' abstractions.

The materialist conception of history

starts from the material production of immediate life and consists in developing the actual process, in seeing the basis of history to be the form of relations linked to the mode of production and created by it (civil society in its various degrees), in expressing this form in its action as a State, in using it to explain the products and forms of consciousness, religion, philosophy, morality etc. ... The environment shapes man and man shapes his environment. This sum of productive forces, capitals and social relations, which each individual and each generation meet with as a datum, is the true substratum of what the philosophers have pictured as 'substance' or 'human essence'; this substratum is not in the least disturbed by the fact that the philosophers have rebelled against it as being 'consciousness of self' or 'unique' ... [DI]

The *German Ideology* also contains a theory of the concrete individual, whose target was Stirner's abstract individualism. For Marx and Engels, alienation, 'to use a term the philosophers can understand', is not a metaphysical notion. The alienation of man in general is only an abstraction. 'Under the name of Man the philosophers have imagined, as an ideal, the individual who is no longer subject to the division of labour.' They have expressed the contradiction between the actual human condition and men's needs abstractly. [DI] The historical and social process which leads from primitive animality to the era of freedom and plenty must be studied empirically. Alienation is one aspect of this process. Up till now there has been, and there still is, a 'reification' of social relations with respect to individuals. Individu-

als alone exist; they are not 'uniques', the same everywhere, with rigid and necessary relations between
them, but real beings, at a particular stage of their
development, joined to each other by relationships
that are complex, concrete and fluid. These individuals can live and develop only within the life of the
human species, within the specifically human life,
that is within a community. Today they must 'sub-
jugate' the alienated and 'reified' powers in actual
practice, so that these can be reintegrated into the
community and into the lives of the individuals freely
joined to that community. In particular they must
transcend the division between the purely individual
life of the individual (his 'private' life) and that part
of his being which is subordinated to the life of
society, to specialization, to the group of which he
forms part (his class) and to the war he wages against
other individuals (competition). Hitherto, in societies
divided into classes, personal interests have developed
in despite of persons 'into class interests which acquire
independence vis-à-vis individual persons and, in their
autonomy, take on the form of general interests,
and as such come into conflict with actual individuals'. [DI] These interests seem to individuals to be
superior to their own individuality, and within such
a framework personal activity can but be alienated,
solidified or reified (*sich versachlichen*) into mechanical operations external to that person. It is as if
there existed within individuals a power whose relationship to them is external or contingent – a series
of social forces 'which determine individuals, control
them and seem to them to be sacred'. These are the
habits and forms of behaviour which the individual believes to be the most profound thing

about him and which in fact come to him from his class.

Stirner did not grasp that the general interest and 'private' interest, the historical process and the actual alienation of the individual, are two aspects of the same development. Their opposition is only momentary, relative to a particular state of society : its division into classes. One of these aspects is constantly being produced, fought against and reproduced by the other. This phase of history has got to be transcended, not in the kind of unity found in Hegel but 'in the materially conditioned destruction of a historical mode of existence of individuals'. [DI]

The isolated individual, Stirner's 'Unique', is an abstraction, just like 'Man in general'. But the fully developed individual, in harmony with the life of the species and the specific content of human life, the free individual in a free community, is not an abstraction. This concrete and complete individual is the supreme instance of thought, the final aim of man's activity.

Abstract individualism leads to a paradoxical result.

Selfishness that is in harmony with itself transforms each man into a secret police state. The spy Reflection watches over every movement of mind and body. Every action, every thought, every vital manifestation becomes a matter for reflection, that is for the police. Selfishness that is in harmony with itself consists in the tearing asunder of man, who is divided into natural instinct and reflection (into creature and creator,

an internal plebs and an internal police force) ...
[DI]

In this way middle-class or lower-middle-class selfishness interposes the mathematics of self-interest between itself and everything else, every desire and
every living being.

Human needs are plastic and go on multiplying,
which is an essential form of progress. We live in a
natural and social environment which allows us to
act and satisfy ourselves 'multilaterally'. It is in any
case absurd to believe that an individual life can be
fulfilled in the form of a single passion, without satis-
fying the whole individual. It is just such a passion
which becomes isolated and abstract in character, or
'alienated'; 'it manifests itself in respect of myself as
an alien power ... The reason for it is not in consciousness but in Being ... in the vital, empirical
development of the individual'. [DI] The individual
thus mutilated develops absurdly. For example,
thought becomes his passion; he becomes involved
in a monotonous reflection on himself which leads
him to declare that his thought is his thought. Now,
as an explanation of thought this is untrue, but it is
only too true as far as this particular individual is
concerned; his thought *is* only his thought.

In the man whose life embraces a wide circle of
diverse activities and practical contacts with the
world, who leads a many-sided life, thought has
the same characteristic of universality as the
other manifestations. Such an individual does
not become fixed as abstract thought, nor does
he need the complicated detours of reflection in

77

order to get from thought to some other vital manifestation.

On the other hand, with a teacher or writer

whose activity is restricted on the one side to an arduous job and on the other to the pleasures of thought ... and whose links with the world are reduced to a minimum as a result of his wretched circumstances, it is inevitable that, if he still feels the need to think, his thought should become as abstract as himself and his life; it will become an unvarying force which, once set in motion, makes it possible for him to enjoy a fleeting pleasure and salvation.

The alienation or, to be more precise, the 'reification' of man's activities is therefore a social fact and also an internal fact, exactly contemporaneous with the formation of the inner or 'private' life of the individual. A psycho-sociology of alienation is possible. We are alienated individuals. All our desires are by nature brutal, one-sided and erratic. They arise haphazardly, infrequently and only when stimulated by some elementary physiological need. And they are brutal in their externalization, repressing other desires and dominating thought itself. The individual may even take a mutilated, one-sided form of activity as his 'vocation', and so be completely led astray and despoiled. Both within and around him the contingent is in control, he is a 'victim of circumstances'. Hitherto freedom has meant simply the opportunity of profiting from chance.

Although certain individuals may see it as a vocation or moral obligation to take action against this state of affairs, such action cannot be purely moral. We have got to achieve a new stage of civilization and culture and enable man to realize his potentialities by altering the conditions of his existence. What is needed is a new 'creation of power'. [DI] Stirner's moral revolt against the existing order, against the social and the 'sacred' in all its forms, is nothing but the canonization of the vague discontent of the lower middle classes. [DI] Only the modern proletariat, which experiences privation, alienation and reification to the full, can will the transcendence of alienation practically (i.e. on the plane of the social praxis, or politically).

The meaning of life lies in the full development of human possibilities, which are constricted and paralysed not by Nature but by the contradictory, class nature of social relations.

Dialectical materialism

In the 1844 *Manuscript*, the *German Ideology* and all the other writings of this period, Hegel's *Logic* is treated with the utmost contempt. Marx and Engels are unsparing in their attacks on this 'esoteric history of the abstract mind', alien to living men, whose elect is the philosopher and whose organ is philosophy. The effect of Hegel's logic is for the son to beget the father, the mind Nature, the concept the thing and the result the principle. [HF]

The Poverty of Philosophy (1846–7) contains passages particularly hostile towards this Hegelian method, which reduces 'everything to the state of logical category, through abstraction and analysis'.

A house becomes a body, then space, then pure quantity. 'All we need to do is leave out of account every distinctive characteristic of the different movements and we arrive at a purely abstract, purely formal movement, at the purely logical formula of movement.' We then imagine that with this logical formula of movement we have discovered the absolute method which explains both movement and things. 'Every object having been reduced to a logical category, and every movement, every act of production to the method, it follows that every combination of products and production, of objects and movement, is reduced to an applied metaphysic.' Hegel's method quite simply abolishes the content, by absorbing it into the abstract form, into Mind and pure Reason. 'What therefore is this absolute method? The abstraction of movement ... the purely logical formula of movement or the movement of pure reason. What does the movement of pure reason consist in? In positing itself, opposing itself, composing itself and formulating itself as thesis, antithesis and synthesis, or alternatively in asserting itself, negating itself and negating its negation.' The dialectical movement (the duplication of every thought into two contradictory thoughts, positive and negative, yes and no, and the fusion of these thoughts) gives rise to groups or series of thoughts and then to Hegel's whole system. 'Apply this method to the categories of political economy and you have the logic and metaphysic of political economy or, in other words, the economic categories which are common knowledge translated into a language that is very uncommon knowledge,' which makes it seem as if they had been freshly hatched in the head of the thinker and as if it were by virtue of the dialectical movement alone that they formed a sequence in which one gives birth to the next. Thus, for Hegel, everything that has ever happened, the whole philosophy of history 'is nothing more than the history of philosophy, and of his particular philosophy'. He believes he is constructing the world in the movement of his thought, whereas he is only systematizing and arranging with his abstract method thoughts that are in everyone's heads. [MP II]

Hegel's dialectic therefore appears to have been damned once and for all. Marx's first accounts of economics (especially *The Poverty of Philosophy*) purport to be empirical. The theory of social contradictions implied in the *Manifesto* of 1848 is inspired by humanism and by 'alienation' in the materialist sense of the term rather than by Hegelian logic. The division of society into classes – social inequality – can be abolished only by those whose material and spiritual 'deprivation' is so profound that they have nothing left to lose.

As yet, therefore, dialectical materialism did not exist, one of its essential elements, the dialectic, having been explicitly rejected. Historical materialism alone had been formulated, whose economic element, invoked as the solution to the problem of man, transforms and transcends philosophy. In their struggle to grasp the content – historical, social, economic, human and practical – Marx and Engels eliminated formal method. The movement of this content involves a certain dialectic : the conflict between classes, between property and deprivation, and the transcending of this conflict. But this dialectic is not linked to a structure of the Becoming which can be

F

expressed conceptually. It is seen as being given practically and verified empirically.

Also at this stage Marx's economic theory had not yet been fully worked out, let alone systematized. All that had appeared were fragmentary and polemical statements of it. For Marx the economic categories were the result of an empirical verification. They remained separate from each other and, as yet, ill-defined. (*The Poverty of Philosophy* confuses labour and labour-power.) The theory of surplus-value, surplus production and crises (together with its political consequences) was not to be worked out until after the economic crises of 1848 and 1857.

We have to wait until the year 1858 to find the Hegelian dialectic being mentioned for the first time non-pejoratively. 'I have been making some jolly discoveries,' Marx wrote to Engels on January 14th, 1858. 'I have thrown overboard the whole theory of profit as it has existed up until now. I have been greatly helped in working out my method because, purely by chance (Freiligrath found some volumes of Hegel which had belonged to Bakunin and sent them to me as a present) I have been browsing through Hegel's *Logic* again. When the time comes to resume this sort of work, I shall very much want to publish two or three papers which will render the rational element of the method which Hegel both discovered and turned into a mystery accessible to common sense.' On February 1st, 1858, Marx drew Engels's attention to the Hegelian pretensions of Lassalle. 'He will learn to his cost that it is not the same thing to bring a science to the point where it can be stated dialectically, and to apply an abstract, ready-made system of logic.'

From this correspondence it follows that the dialectical method was rediscovered and rehabilitated by Marx at the time when he was beginning work on the *Critique of Political Economy* and *Capital*. His elaboration of the economic categories and their internal connections went beyond empiricism and attained the level of a rigorous science – then took on the form of a dialectic.

An important article by Engels (which appeared in 1864 in the *Peuple* of Brussels) on the 'Contribution to the Critique of Political Economy', indicates very precisely the two elements of Marx's mature thought. The materialist conception of history asserts that the conditions men live under determine their consciousness and that

at a certain stage of their development the material forces of production come into conflict with the existing relations of production ... Having been up until this time a form of development of the forces of production, these relations of property are transformed into obstacles ... A form of society never passes away before all the forces of production it may contain have been developed; superior relations of production are never substituted for this form before the conditions for their existence have been incubated in the heart of the old form of society. This is why humanity never sets itself problems it cannot solve ... (From the preface to the 'Contribution')

The other element of Marxian thought, Engels goes on, is the Hegelian dialectic, which is the answer to 'a question which in itself had nothing to do with political economy', to wit the question of method

in general. Hegel's method was unusable in its speculative form. It started from the idea and we must
start from the facts. However, it was the only valid
element in the whole of existing logic. Even in its
idealist form the development of ideas ran parallel
to the development of history.

> If the true relations of things were reversed and
> stood on their heads, their content would still
> pass into philosophy ... Hegel was the first to try
> and show a development in history, an inner law
> ... Marx alone was capable of extracting the
> kernel from Hegel's *Logic* ... and of re-establish-
> ing the dialectical method, freed from its idealist
> wrapping, in the simple form where it becomes
> the exact form of the development of ideas. In
> our view, the elaboration of the method under-
> lying Marx's critique of political economy is a
> result hardly any less important than the fun-
> damental conception of materialism.

The dialectical method thus came to be added to
historical materialism and the analysis of the economic content, once this analysis had been sufficiently
developed to allow and demand a rigorous scientific
expression. The dialectical method, worked out first
of all in an idealist form, as being the activity of the
mind becoming conscious of the content and of the
historical Becoming, and now worked out again,
starting from economic determinations, loses its abstract, idealist form, but it does not pass away. On
the contrary, it becomes more coherent by being
united with a more elaborate materialism. In dialectical materialism idealism and materialism are not

only re-united but transformed and transcended.

'This method starts from the simplest fundamental relations we can find historically, in actual fact, that is economic relations.' [Art. Cit.] This passage answers certain simplistic Marxists as well as most critics of Marxism in advance: economic relations are not the only relations but the simplest ones, the ones found again as 'moments' in complex relations. As currently interpreted, dialectical materialism looks on ideas, institutions and cultures – on consciousness – as a frivolous and unimportant superstructure above an economic substance which alone is solid. True materialism is quite different; it determines the practical relations inherent in every organized human existence and studies them inasmuch as they are concrete conditions of existence for cultures or ways of life. The simple relations, moments and categories are involved, historically and methodologically, in the richer and more complex determinations, but they do not exhaust them. The given content is always a concrete totality. This complex content of life and consciousness is the true reality which we must attain and elucidate. Dialectical materialism is not an economicism. It analyses relations and then reintegrates them into the total movement.

The very fact that these are relations implies the existence of two opposed elements. Each of these elements is considered in itself, and from this examination stems the kind of their mutual relation, of their action and reaction on each other. Antagonisms will be produced requiring a solution ... We shall examine the nature of this solution and shall see that it was obtained by means of the creation of a new relation, whose two conflicting terms we shall have to develop.' [Art. Cit.]

Although Marx never followed up his plan of expounding his dialectical methodology – and although he did not use the words 'dialectical materialism' to describe his doctrine – the elements of his thought are undeniably those conveyed by this term. One can understand why he should have stressed the dialectical form of his account of economics with a certain 'coquetry' as he himself puts it (in the preface to the second edition of *Capital*), having previously come down so hard on all 'metaphysics of political economy'.

His method 'does more than differ from Hegel's method in its fundamentals, it is the direct opposite of it'. Ideas are only things transposed and translated into the heads of men. The Hegelian dialectic has got to be turned inside out if we are to discover the rational kernel beneath the mystical envelope. [K, I, 48] The dialectic is a 'method of exposition', a word to which Marx gives a very powerful meaning. The 'exposition' is nothing less than the complete reconstitution of the concrete in its inner movement, not a mere juxtapositioning or external organization of the results of the analysis. We must start from the content. The content comes first, it is the real Being which determines dialectical thought. 'The object of our method of inquiry is to take possession of matter in its detail, to analyse its various forms of development and to discover its inner laws.' The analysis therefore determines the relations and moments of the complex content. Only then can the movement of the whole be reconstituted and 'exposed'. When the life of the content is reflected in ideas 'we may imagine that we are dealing with an *a priori* construct.' In a general way 'the concrete is concrete because it is the synthesis of several determinations, multiplicity made one. In thought it appears as a process of synthesis, as a result and not as a starting-point, although it is the true starting-point.' [KPO] The analysis of the given reality, from the point of view of political economy, leads to 'general abstract relations' : division of labour, value, money, etc. If we confine ourselves to the analysis we 'volatilize' the concrete representation into abstract determinations, and lose the concrete presupposed by the economic categories, which are simply 'abstract, one-sided relations of an already given concrete and living whole'. This whole must be recovered by moving from the abstract to the concrete. The concrete totality is thus the conceptual elaboration of the content grasped in perception and representation; it is not, as Hegel thought, the product of the concept begetting itself above perception and representation. 'The whole, such as it appears in our brain as a mental whole, is a product of this thinking brain, which takes possession of the world in the only way open to it,' that is by scientific study. The actual datum can therefore remain always present as content and presupposition.

Hegel had made a distinction between the categories – determinations of thought in its immediate relation with objects, intuitions, observations and experiences – and the concept, whose science for him was logic. According to Hegel the concept had a far greater importance and truth than the categories:

the truth of the categories came to them from the concept, since they recur in the latter's systematic inner movement. The materialist dialectic necessarily gives the categories an essential role to play. They have their own truth in themselves, without needing to be attached to the concept in general and its purely logical development. There are specifically economic categories, which result from the relations between the mind and the content, the economic object. Yet the passages quoted above from the Introduction to *The Critique of Political Economy* see the categories as abstractions. The analysis would thus lead to relations essential to the study of the content in question but which would have no existence or truth independently of the whole. What then is the relation of the category to the whole and to the concept of this whole? Is there an economic abstraction, resulting from the subjective application of reflection to the specifically economic facts? How can we reconstitute a concrete whole with elements that have no truth or reality?

It would seem that between starting work on *The Critique of Political Economy* (1857-9) and *Capital* (1867) Marx worked out his conception of the dialectic still more thoroughly. The categories are abstract, inasmuch as they are elements obtained by the analysis of the actual given content, and inasmuch as they are simple general relations involved in the complex reality. But there can be no pure abstraction. The abstract is also concrete, and the concrete, from a certain point of view, is also abstract. All that exists for us is the concrete abstract. There are two ways in which the economic categories have a concrete, objective reality: historically (as moments of the social reality) and actually (as elements of the social objectivity). And it is with this double reality that the categories are linked together and return dialectically into the total movement of the world.

An object, a product of practical activity, answers to a practical need; it has a use-value. Under certain social conditions (as soon as there exist sufficient techniques, a production which exceeds the immediate needs of the producers, means of communication, etc.) the object is involved in exchanges. What producers are doing when they exchange an object can be described in different ways: psychologically, sociologically, economically. As far as the economist is concerned these producers, without being aware of it, are conferring on the object a second existence very different from its materiality. The object enters into new social relations, which it helps to create. This second social existence is abstract yet real. The material object alone exists, yet its value is duplicated, into a use-value and an exchange-value. These two aspects of value are never completely separate, yet they are distinct and contrary. In and through exchange, producers cease to be isolated; they form a new social whole. The exchange of commodities tends to put an end to a natural, patriarchal economy. In relation to individuals this new social whole functions as a superior organism. In particular, it imposes on them a division and distribution of labour in conformity with the sum of the forces of production and the requirements of society. Henceforth producers and groups of producers, in each branch of production, must work in accordance with social demand. If the production of a particular group does not correspond to a demand, or if the productivity of this group falls too far below that of society in general, it is automatically eliminated by its competitors. Society therefore distributes its total labour-power amongst the different branches of production with a certain blind and brutal inevitability. The law of equilibrium of this market society emerges brutally from the general contradiction between producers – their competition. The process which duplicated value into use-value and exchange-value also duplicated human labour. On the one hand there is the labour of living individuals, on the other social labour. Use-values and the labour of living individuals are qualitative and heterogeneous. Exchange value and social labour are quantitative. This quality and quantity are connected yet distinct, and interact on one another. Exchange-value is measured quantitatively : its specific measure is the currency. Quantitative labour is a social mean, wherein all the qualitative features of individual labour vanish bar one, which is common to all forms of labour and makes them commensurable and comparable : every act of production demands a certain length of time. The labour of individuals returns into the social mean by virtue of the labour-time it represents, the objective and measurable period of time it requires. The labour-times of individuals are added up and the total time a society devotes to production is compared with the sum of its products. In this way a social mean is established, which determines the average productivity of the society in question. Then, by a sort of reversal, each individual's labour-time and each product is evaluated – as being an exchange-value – as a fraction of the mean social labour-time (social labour-time, which is abstract and homogeneous, is not to be confused with the unqualified labour of the individual; many critics have made this mistake). Nobody works out this social mean, which arises objectively, spontaneously and automatically from the comparison (equalization) of the individual labour of competing producers. The exchange-value of a product (and the currency is one of these products) is measured by the quantity of social labour it represents. The duplication of value into use-value and exchange-value therefore develops into a complex dialectic, in which we find once again the great laws discovered by Hegel: the unity of opposites and the transformation of quality into quantity and quantity into quality.

Use-value is concrete. Exchange-value, the first and simplest of all the economic categories, obtained from the analysis of the actual economic content, and a starting-point for that movement of thought which seeks to reconstitute the concrete totality, is an abstraction. Yet it is also concrete. With its appearance history has entered on a new phase, and economic development on to a higher level. Exchange-value was at the starting-point of an eminently concrete process: the market economy, which appeared, a qualitative result of a quantitative increase, once the number of producers of commodities and exchanges had increased. Immediately it was formulated, this category reacted on its own pre-conditions, reshaping man's past, pre-forming the future, and playing the role of destiny. It is neither the mechanical sum nor the passive result of the activity of individuals. This activity produces and reproduces it, but the category is something quite new and necessary in relation to individual contingencies; it controls these contingencies and arises out of them as their global and statistical mean.[1] Individuals alone had seemed concrete, then suddenly, faced by the social object – the market with its inexorable laws – to which they are subject and which exerts a 'force of circumstance' over them, they are nothing more than abstractions.

Yet between living individuals there exist only living relations – acts and events. But these become interwoven in a global result or social mean. Once launched on its existence the Commodity involves and envelops the social relations between living men. It develops, however, with its own laws and imposes its own consequences, and then men can enter into relations with one another only by way of products, through commodities and the market, through the currency and money. Human relations seem to be nothing more than relations between things. But this is far from being the case, or rather it is only partly true. In actual fact the living relations between individuals in the different groups and between these groups themselves are made manifest by these relations between things: in money relations and the exchange of products. Conversely, these relations between things and abstract quantities are only the appearance and expression of human relations in a determinate mode of production, in which individuals (competitors) and groups (classes) are in conflict or contradiction. The direct and immediate relations of human individuals are enveloped and supplanted by mediate and abstract relations which mask them. The objectivity of the commodity, of the market and of money is both an appearance and a reality. It tends to function as an objectivity independent of men;

[1] See Hegel: *Wissenschaft der Logik*, bk. III; Engels: *Dialektik und Natur*.

men (and more especially economists) tend to believe in a reality independent of the relations objectified in the abstractions, commodity and money. 'I call this Fetishism, which is attached to the products of labour as soon as they are produced as commodities and which is consequently inseparable from the production of commodities.' [K I] Fetishism is both a mode of existence of the social reality, an actual mode of consciousness and human life, and an appearance or illusion of human activity. Primitive fetishism and magic expressed Nature's dominance over man and the illusory sway of man over Nature. Economic Fetishism expresses the dominance over man of his own products and the illusory sway of man over his own organization and artefacts. Instead of stemming from an ethnographic description, the new Fetishism and fetishized life stems from a dialectical theory of objectivity and the creative activity, of appearance and reality, of concrete and abstract.

In the first place then, exchange-value has an historical reality. At particular points in time it has been the dominant and essential category : in antiquity, in the Middle Ages, in the market economy. In the modern economy it is, in itself, 'antediluvian', no longer anything more than an abstraction, having been transcended. Yet it remains the basis, the fundamental 'moment' which is perpetually being reproduced. But for the perpetual exchange of commodities there could be no world market, no commercial, industrial or financial capital. And it is in modern society that commerce – buying and selling – has reached its greatest possible extent. Like it or not the activity of individuals is exercised within this framework, collides with these limits, and assists in the continual creation of this fundamental category.

Secondly, exchange-value is the very basis of the objectivity of the economic, historical and social process which has led up to modern capitalism. As an essential moment of economic history, exchange-value has accompanied the development of production and of needs, and the broadening of human relations. Spontaneously, men have only an indirect and mystified awareness of this. They do not – they cannot – recognize in the market their own handiwork turning brutally and oppressively against them. They believe in the absolute objectivity, the blind fatality of social facts, which they call destiny or providence. For many modern men, and especially for economists, the laws of the market are absolute, 'natural' laws. Objects or goods have the absolute, natural quality of becoming capital. These men (economists or legislators) sometimes seek to influence these laws by procedures that owe more to magic than to science: economic conferences, speeches, appeals to a mysterious and providential confidence. But to get to know economic phenomena is, on the contrary, to study their objective and substantial process, while at the same time destroying and denying this absolute substantiality by determining it as a manifestation of man's practical activity, seen as a whole (praxis). Because the actual content, and the movement of this content, consists in the living relations of men amongst themselves, men can escape from economic fatalities. Once they have become conscious of it they can transcend the momentary form of their relations; they always have resolved and still can resolve the contradictions of their relations 'by practical methods, with practical energy'.

The study of economic phenomena is not an empirical one, it rests on the dialectical movement of the categories. The basic economic category – exchange-value – is developed and, by an internal movement, gives rise to fresh determinations: abstract labour, money, capital. Each complex determination emerges dialectically from the preceding ones. Each category has a logical and methodological role, it has its place in the explicative whole which leads to the reconstitution of the given concrete totality, the modern world. It also corresponds to an epoch, and the general historical characteristics of the epoch in question – the framework for events and actions – can be deduced by starting from the category essential to it. This theoretical deduction must thus agree with the empirical and specifically historical research into documents, eye-witness accounts and events. The era of the market economy was followed by that of commercial capitalism, industrial capitalism and financial capitalism. Each of these eras is a concrete totality; they are linked together, mingle with one another and are transcended. To each category there corresponds a new degree of economic objectivity, an objectivity at once more real and more apparent: more real because it dominates living men more brutally, more false because it masks men's living relations beneath the deployment of Fetishism. More even than the commodity, money and capital weigh down on human relations from outside, yet they are only the expression and manifestation of these relations. 'In the capital which produces interest, the automatic fetish is perfected; we have money producing money. Nothing at all is left of the past, the social relation is no longer anything more than the

relation of a thing (money or commodity) to itself ...'
Marx was to write in the conclusion to his *Theories on Surplus-Value* (studies intended to form the last volume of *Capital*, which were collected after his death and published in 1904).

To man's activity capital thus appears 'as an objective, alien and autonomous condition'. It becomes 'something at once real and unreal, in which the living relation is included ... It is the form of its reality.' It is in this form that it is developed, exists socially and produces its objective consequences.

The social and historical process therefore has two aspects that cannot be separated. On the one hand it is an increase in the forces of production, an economic and historical determinism – a brutal objectivity. But this objectivity is not self-sufficient, it is not the highest objectivity, that of man's vital activity, consciously producing the human. We must not be taken in by it, like the fetishists; it is only a one-sided determination. The most objective is also and at the same time the most abstract, the most unreal of appearances. From another equally valid and equally true point of view, the social process is the alienation of living men. The economic theory of Fetishism takes up again, raises to a higher level and makes explicit the philosophical theory of alienation and the 'reification' of the individual. His activity, or the product of his activity, appears before him as other, as his negation. The man who acts is the positive element, grounded on itself, of the real and of history. Apart from him there are only abstractions. Man's activity can be alienated only in a fictive substance. Men make their history. It is an illusion that the historical reality should appear external to living men, as an historical, economic or social substance, or as the mysterious subject of the Becoming. The true subject of the Becoming is living man. Yet around and above him the abstractions acquire a strange existence and a mysterious efficacy; Fetishes reign over him.

The first of Marx's great investigations into economics was 'a critique of political economy'. If we want to understand the fundamentals of his thought this word 'critique' must be taken in its widest sense. Political economy, like religion, has got to be criticized and transcended. The 'social mystery' is fetishist and religious in nature. Political economy is a three-fold alienation of man : in the errors of economists, who take the momentary results of human relations to be permanent categories and natural laws; as a science of a substantial object external to man; as a reality and an economic destiny. This alienation is real, it sweeps away living men; yet it is only the manifestation of these men, their external appearance, their alienated essence. For as long as human relations are contradictory (for as long that is as men are divided into classes) the solution of this contradiction will appear and deploy itself as something external, eluding our activity and consciousness : economic mechanisms, States and institutions, ideologies.

'We must rip away the veil from substantial life,' Hegel had written, and this was the programme which Marx was to carry out. Substantial alienation, or reification, denies living men. But they in their turn deny it. By knowledge and by action they disperse the heavy clouds of Fetishism and transcend the conditions that gave birth to it. Marxism is far from asserting that the only reality is economic reality and that there is an absolute economic fatalism. On the contrary, it declares that an economic destiny is relative and provisional, that it is destined to be transcended once men have become aware of their possibilities, and that this transcending will be the essential, infinitely creative act of our own age.

The historical process, that abstract-concrete, develops contradictorily. The mere separation of exchange-value from use-value separates production from consumption, and these two elements of the economic process will diverge until they enter into contradiction. The duplication of value is the most immediate and simplest pre-condition for economic crises, of which, in itself, it establishes the possibility. The capitalist mode of production is particularly contradictory, by virtue of 'its tendency towards the absolute development of the forces of production, a tendency always in conflict with the specific conditions of production within which capital moves.' [K III] The economic crisis makes manifest this contradiction between the power of production (relative surplus-production) and the power of consumption, between the mode of production and the social conditions of production. 'Once the antagonism and contradiction between the relations of distribution and the forces of production have been accentuated, then the moment of the crisis has arrived.' The economic crisis is dialectic. It leads 'normally' to a destruction of forces of production, both men and things. Thus, after a more or less lengthy period of ruin and upheaval, it restores the ratio between the power of consumption and that of production. Only then can the economy come to life again, reproduction be extended and more capital accumulated. As well as expressing the inner contradiction of this society, dominated as it is by the private ownership of the main means of production, the economic crisis also expresses its internal unity. It restores its equilibrium brutally and automatically; it is therefore, in such a system, normal and even normative. It represents the 'force of circumstance' proper to this system. These crises occur periodically, each one being longer and more profound than the last, as an apparently natural catastrophe; by shaking up the system they purge and preserve it. It is not the economic crisis that will destroy this system but the will of men.

Social conditions today are characterized by a dialectical inversion with regard to property. Originally property was a right based on the labour of the person, and on his appropriation of the product of this labour. Today it appears as the right, for those in possession of the means of production, to appropriate the surplus-value, that is the labour-time that has not been paid for. Property today is the negation of private individual property based on personal labour. But it necessarily gives rise to its own negation – the negation of the negation – which 'does not re-establish the private property of the worker, but individual property based on the conquests of the capitalist era: co-operation and the collective ownership of the means of production produced by labour itself.' [K I]

Subjectively, the man who acts, the natural and objective individual, also passes through a contradictory process. Alienation is not a fixed and

99

permanent illusion. The individual is alienated, but as part of his development. Alienation is the objectification, at once real and illusory, of an activity which itself exists objectively. It is a moment in the development of this activity, in the increasing power and consciousness of man. The living individual is the prisoner of outside forces, but these are his forces, his objective content. By overcoming their externality and integrating them, he will achieve his fullest development. Wealth and privation, a religious outlook and concern for man's earthly salvation, an abstract culture and lack of culture, political theory and practical oppression, these have been and still are essential contradictions which tear the human reality apart. Yet wealth in itself is good; abundance of goods and desires makes for a full existence; the State is an organizing power; culture is the highest form of consciousness and life. Fetishes have a content. Fetishism bears on the form, and to transcend it means to discriminate between form and content, to transcend their contradiction and reintegrate the content into the concrete life of men. The enjoyment of riches, organizing power, culture and the sense of community must be reintegrated into the free association of individuals who are both free and conscious of their social content.

Unity of the doctrine

The recent publication of the 1844 *Manuscript* and *The German Ideology* has thrown a new light on the formation and objectives of Marxian thought.

The texts in question did not reveal Marx's humanism, which was already known from *The Holy*

Family, *The Jewish Question* and the *Critique of Hegel's Philosophy of Right*, but they do show how the development of his ideas – his economic theory – did not destroy his concrete humanism but made it richer and explicit.

Dialectical materialism was formed and developed dialectically. Marxian thought began from Hegel's logic and first of all denied this logic in the name of materialism, that is, of a consequent empiricism. The discovery of the natural (material) man of flesh and blood was the first moment of this development. It seemed incompatible with Hegel's Idea and with his absolute method, which constructs its own abstract object. And yet this humanism went further than the materialism of the eighteenth century, which had been based on the early results of the natural sciences; it implied Hegel's theory of alienation and gave alienation a decisive scope, attributing to it both a good and a bad side and determining it as a creative process. In the 1844 *Manuscript*, the theory of alienation is still closer to Hegelian rationalism than to Feuerbach's naturalism. However, it demands that speculative philosophy be transcended, in the name of action and practice; practice is seen as both a beginning and an end, as the origin of all thought and the source of every solution, as a fundamental relation of the living man to Nature and to his own nature. The critical investigation into economics (whose importance Engels was the first to notice) then comes to be naturally integrated with humanism, as being an analysis of the social practice, that is of men's concrete relations with each other and with Nature. The most pressing human problems are determined as economic problems, calling for practical, that is for political solutions, politics being the supreme instance of the social practice, the only means of acting consciously on social relations.

As this humanism becomes more profound it next reveals the dialectical elements it had contained: a dialectic of historical contradictions and the economic categories, a dialectic of 'reification' or alienation. Historical materialism, inasmuch as it is a science of economics, integrates the dialectical method with itself and, raised thereby to a higher level, appears as an application of the general method – the scientific dialectic – to a specific field. After having been denied by Marx, the dialectic joins up again with a more profound materialism; it has itself been freed from its momentary and congealed form: Hegelianism. It has ceased to be the absolute method, independent of the object, and has become the scientific method of exploration and exposition of the object. It discovers its truth by being united with the actual content.

In other words:

(a) The materialist dialectic accords the primacy explicitly to the content. The primacy of the content over the form is, however, only one definition of materialism. Materialism asserts essentially that Being (discovered and experienced as content, without our aspiring to define it *a priori* and exhaust it) determines thought.

(b) The materialist dialectic is an analysis of the movement of this content, and a reconstruction of the total movement. It is thus a method of analysis for each degree and for each concrete totality – for each original historical situation. At the same time it is a synthetic method that sets itself the task of comprehending the total movement. It does not lead to axioms, constancies or permanencies, or to mere analogies, but to laws of development.

(c) Thus understood, the dialectical method therefore constructs the historical and sociological object, while locating and determining its specific objectivity. A brute objectivity of history would be inaccessible, transcendent to the individual mind, the concept and discourse. It would be overwhelming and inexorable in character; allowing itself to be described indefinitely, but without our being able to glimpse any explanatory analysis or effectiveness in it. Conversely, without an object and without objectivity there is no science; every historical or sociological theory which sets out to be a science must establish the reality of its object and define the method which enables it to approach this object. Dialectical materialism satisfies this double requirement of the scientific mind. It establishes the economic objectivity without hypostatizing it, it locates the objective reality of history but straight away transcends it, as being a reality independent of men. It thus introduces living men – actions, self-interest, aims, unselfishness, events and chances – into the texture and intelligible structure of the Becoming. It analyses a totality that is coherent yet many-sided and dramatic.

Is not dialectical materialism therefore both a science and a philosophy, a causal analysis and a world-view, a form of knowledge and an attitude to life, a becoming aware of the given world and a will to transform this world, without any one of these characteristics excluding the other?

The movement and inner content of Hegel's dialectic, between rationalism and idealism, that is, are taken up again in dialectical materialism, which, in one sense, is more Hegelian than Hegelianism. A plurality of different and perhaps even incompatible meanings of the dialectic survived in the speculative dialectic. The dialectic as a method of analysis of the content excluded the dialectic as *a priori* construct, and these two meanings did not fit in very well with the theory of alienation. By positing a total, *a priori* object – absolute knowledge, the system – Hegel went against the content, against the Becoming, against living subjectivity and negativity. Dialectical materialism restores the inner unity of dialectical thought. It dissolves the static determinations attributed by Hegel to the Idea, to knowledge, to religion and to the State. It rejects any speculative construct, any metaphysical synthesis. Thus the different meanings of the dialectic become not only compatible but complementary. The dialectical method epitomizes the investigation of the historical development, it is the highest consciousness which living man can have of his own formation, development and vital content. Categories and concepts are elaborations of the actual content, abbreviations of the infinite mass of particularities of concrete existence. The method is thus the expression of the Becoming in general and of the universal laws of all development. In themselves these laws are abstract but they can be found in specific forms in all concrete contents. The method begins from the logical sequence of fundamental categories, a sequence by virtue of which we can recover the Becoming, of which they are the abridged expression. This method permits the analysis of particularities and specific situations, of the original concrete contents in the various spheres. It becomes the method that will guide the transformation of a world in which the form (economic, social, political or ideological) is not adequate to the content (to man's actual and potential power over Nature and his own artefacts) but enters into contradiction with it.

The Third Term is therefore the practical solution to the problems posed by life, to the conflicts and contradictions to which the praxis gives birth and which are experienced practically. The transcending is located within the movement of action, not in the pure time-scale of the philosophical mind. Wherever there is a conflict there may – but it is not inevitable – appear a solution which transforms the opposed terms and puts an end to the conflict by transcending them. It is up to the analysis to determine this solution, up to experience to release it, and up to action to realize it. Sometimes there is no solution : no social group was capable of putting an end to the economico-political contradictions of the Roman world in its decadence.

The relation between the contradictories ceases therefore to be a static one, defined logically and then found again in things – or negated in the name of a transcendent absolute. It becomes a living relation, experienced in existence. Several of Hegel's illustrations of the reciprocal determination of contradictories (*summum jus, summa injuria* – the way East is also the way West, etc.) become insufficient. The opposed terms are energies, or acts. The unity of the contradictories is not only an interpenetration of concepts, an internal scission, it is also a struggle, a dramatic relation between energies which are only by virtue of one another and cannot exist except one against the other. Thus Master and Slave or, if one prefers, the different species of animals. This struggle is a tragic relation, in which the contradictories are produced and support one another mutually, until either one of them triumphs and they are transcended or else they destroy each other. Taken in all its objectivity, the contradiction is fluid, and the logical relation is only its abstract expression. The transcending is action and life, the victory of one of the two forces which overcomes the other by transforming it, transforming itself and raising the content to a higher level.

The problem of man – or, more precisely, the problem of modern society, of the 'social mystery' and its transcending – is central for dialectical materialism, which has appeared in this society at its appointed hour, as a scientific expression of its reality, its multiform contradictions and the potentialities it contains.

However, in order to elucidate modern industrial society, the analysis must go back to older societies. These it determines in their relation to the concrete totality as given today, inasmuch as they are original totalities that have been transcended, that is in the only historical reality that we can conceive of or determine. In the past this analysis finds, under specific forms, certain relations (such as that between Master and Slave for example, which Marx called 'the exploitation of man by man') or else typical modes of thought or social existence, such as Fetishism. Dialectical materialism's field cannot therefore be restricted to the present day, it extends over the whole of sociology. But Nature itself exists for us only as a content, in experience and human practice.

The dialectical analysis is valid for any content, it expresses the connection between the elements or moments of all Becoming. By incorporating the experimental sciences (physical, biological, etc.) and using them to verify itself, it can therefore discover, even in Nature, quality and quantity, quantity turning into quality, reciprocal actions, polarities and discontinuities, the complex but still analysable Becoming.

The sciences of Nature are specific. They recognize and study as such natural, physical, biological, etc., polarities or oppositions. They use the concept as a 'trick' in order to study and modify qualities through the mediation of quantities, but they are never able to overcome these oppositions. Social science on the other hand examines the oppositions so as to overcome them. The sciences of Nature and the social sciences are specifically creative, each of them having its own method and objectives. However, the laws of the human reality cannot be entirely different from the laws of Nature. The dialectical chain of fundamental categories may therefore have a universal truth. It was only with great caution that Marx embarked on this path (as in his application of the dialectical method to economics). However, *Capital* shows how, in Marxian thought, the concrete dialectic is extended to Nature [K I], an extension carried on by Engels in *Dialectics of Nature*. Their *Correspondence* at this period (1873–4) shows that Marx followed Engels's endeavour closely and approved of it.

Thus dialectical materialism is made universal and acquires the full dimensions of a philosophy: it becomes a general conception of the world, a

Weltanschauung and hence a renewal of philosophy.

For the materialist dialectician, universal inter-dependence (*Zusammenhang*) is not a formless tangle, a chaos without structure. It is only the decline of speculative thought since Hegel that has dissociated the determinations and devalued the structural elements of the Becoming: quantity, discontinuity, relative nothingness. Dialectical materialism rescues the human mind from falling back into confusion and one-sidedness. The totality of the world, the infinite-finite of Nature, has a determinable structure, and its movement can become intelligible for us without our having to attribute it to an organizing intelligence. Its order and structure emerge from reciprocal action, from the complex of conflicts and solutions, destructions and creations, transcendings and eliminations, chances and necessities, revolutions and involutions. Order emerges from the Becoming; the structure of the movement is not distinct from the movement. Relative disorders prepare a new order and make it manifest.

All reality is a totality, both one and many, scattered or coherent and open to its future, that is, to its end. Between 'moments' there cannot exist either a purely external finality or a purely internal one, either a harmony or mechanical collisions. Being elements of a totality, having been transcended and maintained within it, limited by each other and yet reciprocally determined, they are the 'ends' one of another. There exist ends without finality. Each moment contains other moments, aspects or elements that have come from its past. Reality thus overflows the mind, obliging us to delve ever deeper into it – and especially to be ever revising our principles of identity, causality and finality and making them more thorough. Being determines our consciousness of Being, and the being of our thought determines our reflection on our thought. The reality is Nature, a given content, yet one that can be apprehended in its infinite richness by the mind which moves forward, based on the praxis, and becomes more and more penetrating and supple, tending as if towards a mathematical limit (to which we are for ever drawing nearer but have never reached), towards absolute knowledge, or the Idea.

The dialectic, far from being an inner movement of the mind, is real, it precedes the mind, in Being. It imposes itself on the mind. First of all we analyse the simplest and most abstract movement, that of thought that has been stripped as far as possible of all content. In this way we discover the most general categories and how they are linked together. Next, this movement must be connected up with the concrete movement, with the given content. We then become aware of the fact that the movement of the content or of Being is made clear for us in the laws of the dialectic. The contradictions in thought do not come simply from thought itself, from its ultimate incoherence or impotence, they also come from the content. Linked together they tend towards the expression of the total movement of the content and raise it to the level of consciousness and reflection.

Our quest for knowledge cannot be thought of as having been terminated by dialectical logic; quite the reverse, it must acquire a fresh impetus from it. The dialectic, a movement of thought, is true only in a mind that is in motion. In the form of a general theory of the Becoming and its laws, or of a theory of knowledge, or of concrete logic, dialectical materialism can only be an instrument of research and action, never a dogma. It does not define, it locates the two elements of human existence: Being and consciousness. It places them in order: Being (Nature) has priority, but consciousness comes first for man. Whatever has appeared in time can be erected, by man and for man, into a superior value. Nor, as a doctrine, can dialectical materialism be enclosed within an exhaustive definition. It is defined negatively, by being opposed to those doctrines which limit human existence, either from without or within, by subordinating it to some external existence or else by reducing it to a one-sided element or partial experience seen as being privileged and definitive. Dialectical materialism asserts that the equalization of thought and Being cannot be reduced to an idea, but must be achieved concretely, that is in life, as the concrete power of the mind over Being.

Dialectical thinking has never ceased to evolve nor new aspects of it to appear, both in the lifetime and the writings of Marx and Engels, and since. Every truth is relative to a certain stage of the analysis and of thought, to a certain social content. It preserves its truth only by being transcended. We must go on constantly deepening our awareness of the content and extending the content itself. In the past as in the present, our knowledge has been limited by the limitation of the content and of the social form. Every doctrine, and this includes dialectical materialism, stems from this limitation, which is not that of the human mind in general but the limitation of man's present state. It is at the precise moment when it becomes aware of its own dialectical nature that thought must distinguish with the utmost care what, in the dialectical movement of ideas, comes from the actual content and what from the present form of thought. The exposition of dialectical materialism does not pretend to put an end to the forward march of knowledge or to offer a closed totality, of which all previous systems had been no more than the inadequate expression. However, with our modern awareness of human potential and of the problem of man, the limitation of thought changes in character. No expression of dialectical materialism can be definitive, but, instead of being incompatible and conflicting with each other, it may perhaps be possible for these expressions to be integrated into an open totality, perpetually in the process of being transcended, precisely in so far as they will be expressing the solutions to the problems facing concrete man.

For man, the relation of a particular reality to the total movement takes the form of a Problem. There is a problem whenever the Becoming carries thought and activity along and orientates them by forcing them to take account of new elements: at the moment when the Solution is tending, so to speak, to enter into reality and demanding the consciousness and the action which can realize it. It is in this sense that humanity only sets itself problems it is capable of solving. The resolution of contradictions in the transcending thus takes on its full practical significance.

The solution – the Third Term – is not an attitude of the mind. There is no substitute for practical contact with things, or effective co-operation with the demands and movements of the content.

In human terms, the energy of creation is extended and made manifest in and through the Praxis, that is the total activity of mankind, action and thought, physical labour and knowledge. The Praxis is doubly creative: in its contact with realities, hence in knowledge, and in invention or discovery. Dialectical materialism seeks to transcend the doctrines which reduce the mind's activity to becoming acquainted with what has already been achieved, or which recommend it to hurl itself into the void of mystical exploration. Experience and reason, intelligence and intuition, knowing and creating, conflict with one another only if we take a one-sided view of them.

The Praxis is where dialectical materialism both starts and finishes. The word itself denotes, in philosophical terms, what common sense refers to as 'real life', that life which is at once more prosaic and more dramatic than that of the speculative intellect. Dialectical materialism's aim is nothing less than the rational expression of the Praxis, of the actual content of life – and, correlatively, the transformation of the present Praxis into a social practice that is conscious, coherent and free. Its theoretical aim and its practical aim – knowledge and creative action – cannot be separated.

In Hegel, the inferior moments had co-existed with the superior ones, in the eternity of the Idea and the system. In this way time, history and freedom had become unreal again, having allowed themselves to be arranged into a schema that included all the established forms of law, of customs and of consciousness. In dialectical materialism negativity is more profoundly positive and dynamic in character. The Third Term, the triumphant outcome of a conflict, transforms the content of the contradiction by re-assuming it; it lacks the conservative solemnity of the Hegelian synthesis. Only in this way can there be a real movement, a dramatic history and action, creation and development, liberation and liberty. The rectilinear schema of the Becoming is too simple, Hegel's triangular one too mechanical. In dialectical materialism the static representation of time is replaced by a vital and directly experienced notion of succession, of the action which eliminates and creates. Man can thus, perfectly rationally, set himself an objective which is both a transcending and a coming to fruition.

In Hegel, finally, the idea and the mind appear to produce themselves only because they already are. History comes to look like a bad joke. At the end of the Becoming all we find is the spiritual principle of the Becoming, which is thus only a repetition, an absurd illusion. The ordeal and misfortunes of consciousness have a ritual, magic action which causes absolute Mind to descend amongst us. But this Hegelian Mind always remains oddly narcissistic and solitary. In its contemplation of itself it obscures the living beings and dramatic movement of the world.

According to dialectical materialism men can and must set themselves a total solution. Man does not exist in advance, metaphysically. The game has not already been won; men may lose everything. The transcending is never inevitable. But it is for this precise reason that the question Man and of Mind acquires an infinite tragic significance, and that those who can sense this will give up their solitude in order to enter into an authentic spiritual community.

II

THE PRODUCTION OF MAN

'Inasmuch as he is a natural being, man is given,' says the *Manuscript* of 1844. At the starting-point of his 'production' therefore we find biological and material Nature, with all its mystery and tragedy. Transformed yet present, this Nature will constantly be appearing in the content of human life. Nature, Being that is, can be explored and expressed poetically, plastically or scientifically. If it were defined, both art and science would become redundant and their autonomy and movement abolished; such a definition would simply be a metaphysical abstraction. The modern mind is only just beginning to sense the depth of the natural 'will-to-live', with its contrasts and ambivalences: its intimate blend of aggressiveness and sympathy, its tumultuous energies and its periods of calm, its destructives furies and its joy. What do they conceal or signify, these biological energies which the Reason must organize and pacify but not destroy? Perhaps, as Hegel and the embryologists believed, they contain the whole past of organic life. No doubt they also transform profoundly their inorganic and organic elements; man's instincts are no longer the same as the corresponding instincts in animals. Our biological energies cannot be determined only by the past of the species, but also by the future they contain within them. To start with, Man was a biological possibility, although this possibility was able to be actualized only after a long struggle, in which Man has increasingly assumed responsibility for his own Being. His activity becomes power and will; painfully, he acquires consciousness. Inasmuch as he is knowledge and existence in the flesh, he becomes the living Idea of Nature. But he does not cease to belong to Nature, his energies are immersed in those of Nature, where they are renewed and destroyed. These energies are also perhaps a refinement as well as, from certain points of view, an exhaustion of the fundamental energies. The Becoming is multiform: evolution, revolution, involution – a descent seen from one side, an ascent seen from another.

The role of philosophical thought is to eliminate premature explanations, those limitative positions which would prevent us from penetrating and possessing the formidable content of our being. All we can say is that Nature is not inert – and that it is not an already real 'soul' or spirit; that we must not picture it as a brute externality or object (or sum of objects), nor as a pure internality or subject (or sum of subjects), because Nature is presupposed in the birth and appearance of subject and object. The best picture we can have of Nature 'in itself', independent of ourselves, is a negative one, no doubt: Nature is 'indifferent', which does not mean that it is hostile or brutally alien to us, but rather undifferentiated in relation to the object and subject of our own experience.

Inasmuch as he is a natural being, man contains a multiplicity of instincts, tendencies and vital forces. As such, he is passive and limited. The objective need of a natural, flesh-and-blood being requires an object

that is also natural. The objects of man's natural instincts (hunger, sexual instinct) as such are outside
him and independent of him. He depends on them.
His need and vital force are thus transformed into
powerlessness and privation.

The relation between a being and its 'other' is thus
given in Nature and experienced 'existentially' by
natural man as externality and dependence. Since he
has other beings for his object, this man is an object
for other beings. He is at once a subject and an
object which are opposed yet inseparable : a material
subject, objectively given in his organism and elementary biological consciousness, and thus containing a
relation with other beings who are, for him, the objects of his desire, but, in themselves, subjects; a
material object for these other beings. The fact that
he is thus an object exposes natural man to the de-
signs and aggressions of other living beings. However, a being who was not objective would be an
absurdity (an *Unding*, says the *Manuscript* of 1844).
He would be alone, in an unbearable metaphysical
solitude. We cease to be alone not when we are with
someone else but when we are ourselves someone
else : another reality than ourselves for ourselves –
another reality than the object for itself. A meeting
of pure subjects (monads) would not draw them out
from their solitude. A being who is not the object
of a desire for another being has no determinable
existence. 'As soon as I have an object, that being has
me for object.' [M 1844]

The natural being therefore has his nature outside
himself, and this is how he participates in Nature. In
this fundamental experience Nature is determined for
us as an externality of elements; but, as Hegel said,

the most external is also the most internal. Natural beings are closely linked and dependent on each other even in their externality, and in their struggles against each other. Natural man as such is passive. Inasmuch as he feels this passivity, that is, the thrust of his desire together with the impotence of that desire, he becomes passionate. 'Passion,' says Marx, 'is an essential force in the man tended towards his object.' Passion is thus given its place; it cannot be condemned by the reason, because the passionate man derives his strength from the most profound energies of Nature. And yet passion as such must be only the basis and starting-point of Power. Power no longer depends on the object, it dominates and contains its object: the objectivity of Nature is no longer anything more than its limit and its end.

For man is not only a being of Nature, he is also human. In and through man Nature is divided and opposed to itself, and enters into a conflict with itself more profound than all its previous contrasts and all the conflicts between individuals or biological species. Man, a being of Nature, turns and fights against Nature. For him, Nature is the primal source, the mother; yet it is nothing more than the given substance on which he acts. Inasmuch as it is external Nature is even his death and his tomb. This other 'existential' experience, to use a modern term, is equally fundamental. Human objects are no longer immediately natural objects. Specifically human feelings, such as manifest themselves objectively, are no longer the natural, human objectivity, brute desire or immediate sensibility. Nature ceases to be present immediately and adequately to man. Like every natural being man must be born. His history is the act of his birth, his coming into being within Nature – and yet outside and against Nature. In the course of this history man erects himself above Nature and slowly brings it under control. 'History is the natural history of man,' says Marx. But this birth is a transcending, and an increasingly conscious transcending. By acting man modifies Nature, both around and within him. He creates his own nature by acting on Nature. He transcends himself in Nature and transcends Nature in himself. By shaping it to his own requirements he modifies himself in his own activity and creates fresh requirements for himself. He forms himself and grasps himself as a power by creating objects or 'products'. He progresses by resolving in action the problems posed by his action.

'The negativity of the object and its transcending thus have a positive significance.' Object and subject are equally positive and objective. It is in order to attain to the object which is outside it that the activity of the subject posits new objects and transcends its natural dependence vis-à-vis objects. Activity thus posits itself as an object: it attains to itself, becomes conscious of itself and acts on itself through the object. It transcends the opposition between subject and object by recovering itself in this objectivity that is superior to natural objectivity.

The one-sidedness of philosophical attitudes has been determined by the limitation of their first step. Idealism, which began with pure activity, independent of its content, led necessarily to a 'formalization' of this activity. Positivism, empiricism or even ordinary materialism started by positing the object, datum or fact independently of activity; they therefore ignored this activity and limited actual Being. A philosophical method which sets out to express man's activity in its completeness must start from a richer notion than that of the brute object or pure activity. The notion of the product represents a higher unity and 'epitomizes activity'. [M 1844]

Analysis of the Product

In any product, however trivial (this table, that hammer, that tree in the garden), the subjective and objective aspects, the activity and the thing, are intimately linked. These are isolated objects that have been separated from Nature. They have definite contours and can be measured from different points of view. They have names that enter into human discourse. The word and the concept finally fix the object, and immobilize it by separating it from Nature.

And yet these products still remain objects of Nature. Nature does not provide a raw material hostile to form; the raw material itself indicates the form the object may receive.

Every product – every object – is therefore turned in one direction towards Nature, and in another towards man. It is both concrete and abstract. It is concrete in having a given substance, and still concrete when it becomes part of our activity, by resisting or obeying it, however. It is abstract by virtue of its definite, measurable contours, and also because it can enter into a social existence, be an object amongst other similar objects and become the bearer of a whole series of new relations additional to its substantiality (in language, or else in the quantitative evaluation of society as a commodity).

Let us examine a very simple case of action being applied to a fragment of matter. Every productive action works to detach a definite object from the enormous mass of the material universe. An object is determinate precisely to the extent that it has been isolated. Anything which restores its relations with its material context and reintegrates it into Nature destroys it as a product or as a human object: the rust on my hammer, for example. In order to be an object and, as such, usable, the hammer must stand out with the utmost clarity of outline and practical reality against the indefinite background of the universe. It is 'abstract', but with an abstraction which is a practical, concrete force.

Some men lift a heavy load. In this simple action the reality of the object governs the activity directly. The shape of the load, its volume, the direction it has got to be moved in, are the objective conditions which the action obeys. Moreover the number of men able to help and their physical strength enter as determining elements into the sequence of synchronized movements which will lead to the load being shifted. By virtue of a reciprocal adaptation of men and object, the activity of this human group will acquire a form, a structure and a rhythm. These remarks can be extended from a very simple case like this to very complex ones: the manufacture of an object, a laboratory experiment, etc. Every time human effort is applied to a 'product', a concrete unity is formed between subject and object, looked at practically. The subject and object are not merged, neither are they abstractly distinct; they are opposed in a certain relationship. They form a clearly determined dialectical whole.

The 'product' need not be thought of exclusively in one place or at one moment of time. A sequence of phenomena can equally well be seen as a product. I put some water on the fire. The container protects the liquid from all the outside disturbances which might hinder the desired result. The combination: fire, container, liquid, must be considered as a product of the action, likewise the successive series of phenomena: the rise in the temperature of the liquid, its coming to the boil. This series is isolated in time, just as the combination of objects is isolated in space. Such a grouping of phenomena, 'consolidated' in time, is known in scientific terms as a determinism. From one point of view this series is real, material and concrete, from another it is 'abstract' in the most precise sense of that word, since to ab-stract means to separate or detach. The starting-point for this abstraction is not in the mind, but in the practical activity; the essential characteristics of sense-perception cannot be correctly deduced from an analysis of thought, but from an analysis of the productive activity and of the product. Abstraction is a practical power.

All production presupposes the organism: the hand, the eye, the brain. It also presupposes the need. Organism and need are both plastic. Man's tendencies are not given right from the start in all their clarity, power and rationality. The product which corresponds to a tendency helps to fix it, to make it conscious and differentiate it. It reacts both on it and on the organism. Man's hand, his eye and his brain are shaped and perfected, in both the individual and the species, by the use he makes of them.

All production presupposes other determinations

of the practical activity too, and especially an instrument or a technique. The instrument enables us to act on objective reality. It is itself an objective reality, an object of Nature. It does not act on Nature from outside but as one fragment of Nature reacting on other fragments.

We might try from this point of view to classify instruments and distinguish between:

(*a*) Those instruments which enable us to detach certain fragments from Nature. In relation to the interdependence of natural phenomena these have a destructive or abstractive character. Examples are the pick-axe, the hammer or the arrow – pure quantity and quality, geometric space, etc.

(*b*) Those instruments which serve to preserve the fragments thus obtained, to protect them in their isolation and to orientate the determinisms subtracted from Nature. Examples: the paint which prevents ironwork from going rusty, containers of any sort, substantives. Indeed, in one sense, language, from the brief word of command up to scientific discourse, is an instrument.

(*c*) Those instruments which then enable us to fashion the fragments that have been maintained in their isolation.

(*d*) Finally, all the results of man's activity, to the extent that they serve to satisfy a need.

Such a classification generalizes the notion of instrument. A house is an instrument, with a certain efficacy in time and space, likewise the community of those working together for a common purpose, and likewise, finally, geometric and social space, clock-time, etc.

A technique is the combination of movements and

operations aimed at a certain result, a combination that is then constituted into a determinate series, itself isolated (determining because it is determined) exactly like an instrument or object.

It must be noted that as thus defined the technique is a moment of the activity, not the whole of it. It is determined, constituted and 'consolidated' as the experiment proceeds. The technique as such therefore is not the originator of the product or of the determinations of the product such as abstraction, significance, value or the relation of the object to the need, the organism and the activity. The technique is formed, it is a result. It is not conscious at the outset and only afterwards is it described and handed on orally. Neither physical techniques nor mental ones are directly understood, right from the beginning. Hence the discoveries of the ethnographers, who have established the juxtaposition in the primitive mind of correct techniques along with strange interpretations of them; oddly enough this surprises them. As if the same juxtaposition could not be found in ourselves, in our own day and age, in relation to physical or even to intellectual techniques: 'inspiration', the mystery of 'creation', etc.

At a very advanced stage, once a large number of techniques have become conscious and been handed on explicitly, once both their specific and their general features are known, once particular techniques such as logic have been consolidated and have provided consciousness with a skeleton, then and only then do we become precisely aware of activity and techniques. Originally, consciousness was, so to speak, located inside the thing, inside the result of the action and inside the objective form given to the product. We discover what we are in what we do. The activity involved in production proceeds first of all hesitantly, by trials and errors that are then rectified. Gradually, the operation itself is consolidated and becomes a technique, after which active man examines his technique with a view to improving it and drawing from it conclusions concerning the properties of the object. He goes from the product to himself, then from himself to the product. Consciousness is formed practically, through activity crystallizing into set methods and procedures, far more than through any withdrawal or retreat on the part of the subject. In this way a painter tests himself out and discovers himself in his earliest attempts, after which he perfects his technique and modifies his style. It would be absurd to suppose that a painter might develop his gift and become conscious of it without actually putting brush to canvas; for him, painting is not merely an excuse, an occasional manifestation of a hidden talent which existed beforehand. Yet such is the hypothesis formulated by idealism about Mind.

The activities of integration

The analysis of the isolated product can be compared with the philosophical analysis of the understanding or *Verstand*. The production of isolated objects, which separates these objects and determines aspects and properties of them, contains the principal characteristics of the *Verstand*, in that it is an intellectual activity which isolates and defines, which works to express the particular significance of objects and strives to become a technique of thought (grammar,

technique of analysis, formal logic). The understanding is the function of the distinct, the individual and
the instant, of the praxis on the scale of the individual or the isolated object – of the practical objective.

Consideration of the isolated object is only a first
step for thought; the fundamental operation of
philosophy has always been the reconstruction of
the whole. Thinking man has always sensed that the
isolated object was inconceivable by itself, that the
abstractive activity itself must also be comprehended,
that is, linked to the complex of the conditions
that determine it and the aims it pursues. He has
always sensed therefore that the initial datum, that
is the whole, must be recovered, by 'comprehending'
it or bringing it under the control of the reason. The
intuitive or primitive mentality preserves a keen
awareness of this whole; whenever it pictures objects
or causal series to itself it feels the need to reintegrate
these products immediately into the totality.

Philosophy has always sought to effect the conscious 'integration' of the element into the totality.
But in the attempt several forms of sophism become
possible. We may look for the principle of integration
in man's activity, seen as a mechanical sum of abstract operations, or else as leading to a determinate
technique such as formal logic. A philosophy which
seeks to reconstitute the whole in this way is doomed
to take an abstract view of the activity's special
operations at the precise moment when it wants to
transcend abstraction and attain the concrete and
the totality. This is what happens in classical idealism.

We may also try to attain the totality on 'this
side' of the abstractive activity, by omitting this
activity: by returning via the imagination towards

a stage previous to the activity, into the domain, that is, of muddled intuitions, on the level of the primitive mentality. This form of 'intuitive' thinking ignores the data of the problem. Starting from a problem posed by the existence of a productive activity of abstraction and by the demand for a higher unity, it quite simply denies this abstractive activity. Such doctrines (intuitionism, primitivism, crude wholism) offer an odd mixture of intellectual sophistication and summary anti-intellectualism.

The integration has got to be carried out consciously and correctly, without leaving any aspect of the problem out of account. The isolated product must be restored to the complex of its relations. The isolation of an object of Nature (its logical identity with itself) can only be a limit, a final aim which our activity can never wholly achieve however hard it tries. An object is isolated or consolidated only in one of its aspects, and only through the mediation of another object itself not wholly isolable (the house that gives me shelter, a tree in the garden, a field of corn). In a whole series of other aspects objects remain immersed in the vast movement of the world. The mind which takes this isolation and consolidation of objects to be an accomplished fact is falling into the error of mechanism; instead of an integration it is performing a summation, and a summation of products, moreover, as if these were natural beings and as if it were possible to recover Nature by adding them together.

We must move from the isolated product to the sum of products and, simultaneously, from consideration of this fragmentary activity to that of the creative activity as a whole. This integration is a fundamental operation both in general philosophy and in various specific sciences, in which a change of scale must be effected in order to get from the element to the whole. Political economy thus demands that we move on from the particular commodity to the market: from the viewpoint of the isolated producer to the examination of production and productivity as a whole. This change of viewpoint is the correlative of a profound change in the nature of the phenomenon. Confusion between the two scales leads to those errors current amongst economists who, without being aware of it, fetishize the whole, by picturing it to themselves as outside and above the elementary phenomena, accepted in their isolation. In sociology and history too, we must pass from the psychological and individual viewpoint to that of the social whole. And in the natural sciences analogous operations might be found, by means of which – thanks to a change of scale – we can move from the elementary phenomenon up to the statistical result: the global mean.

As far as the analysis of human activity is concerned, such an operation is possible only because the whole exists concretely and pre-exists its elements; in one sense these elements are real, 'in themselves', as moments of the whole, but in another sense they are simply abstractions in relation to the whole. The social whole is given as a practical organization or Praxis.

This change of scale corresponds to the philosophical transition from the *Verstand* (understanding) to the *Vernunft* (reason), and gives the order for this transition. Integration is not a speculative fantasy. The unity of the world, which is shattered in one way by the activity of fragmentation, by the production of isolated objects and the consolidation (material or intellectual) of particular causal series, is continued – although specifically – on the human plane. Every activity is a co-operation. Human needs are not absolutely separate from each other either in time or in space, either in the individual or in the group. One technique gives birth to another, one technique perfects another, etc. Reason is the function of the movement, of the whole, of the total life and of the transcending.

The objective world of man is a world of products forming a whole: what we traditionally refer to as the world of sense-perception. This social world is laden with affective or representative meanings which extend beyond the instant, the separate object, the isolated individual. In this sense the most trivial object is the bearer of countless suggestions and relationships; it refers to all sorts of activities not immediately present in it. For child and adult alike, objects are not merely a momentary material presence, or the occasion of a subjective activity; they provide us with an objective social content. Traditions (technical, social, spiritual) and the most complex qualities are present in the humblest of objects, conferring on them a symbolic value or 'style'. Each object is a content of consciousness, a moment.

When the sum of objects is thought of as a whole, products acquire a higher meaning which they do not have when they are seen in isolation. Man's activity, examined on the scale of the Praxis, receives fresh determinations, that is, a higher form and content. A country is a product of human activity, since it has been fashioned by successive generations. The very face of the earth, the landscape and the whole of Nature such as it exists for us at this moment, are a product with the two aspects implied in that term, the subjective and the objective.

Human consciousness thus appears in its relation to the sum of products. This relation is a profound one even where an artist is concerned, who creates himself and grasps himself in his work and in the succession of his artefacts. It becomes more profound still when a historical community is concerned. The activity of production and social labour must not be understood in terms of the non-specialized labour of the manual worker (although this labour does have its function within the whole); it must be understood on the scale of humanity. Production is not trivial. Labour must not be reduced to its most elementary form but, on the contrary, thought of in accordance with its higher forms: total labour then takes on its creative or 'poetic' meaning. The creation that is pursued in the Praxis, through the sum of individual acts and existences, and throughout the whole development of history, is the creation of man by himself. 'The so-called history of the world is nothing other than the production of man through human labour.' [M]

Within Nature, this vast complex, the world of products or total Instrument, is interposed between Man and Nature; it is an object of Nature, but turned towards man. Without this complex of tools and techniques men are nothing. Yet the human cannot be the utilitarian or instrumental. Whenever men become instruments, whenever the ends of human activity are purely utilitarian (even though these may be disguised by the ideologies used to justify them), then man's condition becomes inhuman. Human beings come to think of themselves as the instruments of transcendental powers: of destinies or divinities. In order to resolve this contradiction between the instrumental existence of *homo faber* and human demands for freedom, some philosophers resort to a transcendency: man will realize himself at a later date, in another life, or on a plane other than the terrestrial – that of mystical 'salvation'. While he waits to be finally liberated man obeys the destiny laid down for him by the transcendent power. Such doctrines restore, even more cruelly, the instrumental mentality they had set out to transcend. There is only one answer that has a positive significance: the activity that turns man into an instrument represents a contradiction within the human which can and must be overcome.

Instruments are not a form imposed on Nature from outside, as abstract categories might be. They are not a prison for man, a rampart between him and Nature. A tropical forest or a storm at sea are purely cosmic; the man who falls victim to such forces is powerless and isolated, outside Nature because he is the victim of Nature. But a landscape that has been humanized – a house built in this landscape in an appropriate style – shows man in Nature, having reconciled himself with it precisely by appropriating it.

The highest consciousness is one of man in Nature, of Nature as different from man yet conditioning his existence. Man's higher consciousness therefore is not one of instruments or techniques, nor a pure consciousness of himself as a subjectivity external to Nature. It expresses a natural life that has been humanized, organized, and thereby intensified since in animals natural life is limited organically, reduced to elementary and incompatible tendencies which vanish the moment they are satisfied.

Industry is the real historical relation between Nature, and hence also the natural sciences, and man; this is why, if we think of it as an exoteric unveiling of the essential forces of man, we can also understand the human essence of Nature, or the natural essence of men; the natural sciences then renounce their abstract and material, or rather idealist, tendency; they become the basis of a science of man, just as, at the present time, they have already become (albeit in an alienated form) the basis of a truly human life. The idea of one basis for life and another for science is false. Nature, such as it becomes in human history ... is the nature of man. [M][1]

In the course of his history, the human being becomes isolated in one sense from Nature, yet in this way he contracts with it a more profound relationship and a higher unity. Man is a naturally limited being who behaves as a whole, who becomes an active subject, a spontaneous Life working to consolidate himself and raise himself up. Man, a finite being who opens up infinite possibilities for himself, is capable of raising himself to a higher degree of

[1] For the last hundred years, as Marx had foreseen, the sciences have been moving towards unity; the natural sciences have been fertilized by becoming aware of the human reality (theory of the struggle for life, historical consciousness, statistical science, etc.).

existence and of looking down on the point from which he started. Man is a movement which is constantly turning back to its starting-point in order to re-assume it and raise it to an ever higher level, a being who contains his entire Becoming within himself and gradually brings it under control. His limitation and abstraction are transformed into a source of power; it is in fact the most limited thing about him – his abstract understanding, the ability to immobilize objects and instants, instruments and concepts, in their separateness – which becomes the principle of this increasing power. Man's consciousness expresses his authority over things, but also his limitation, since it can be attained only by way of abstraction and logic, and in the consciousness of the theoretical man who is alien to Nature. Consciousness expresses therefore both the finitude and infinitude of man. Herein lies his inner contradiction, which forces him constantly to deepen and transcend himself. Herein too lies his drama, his misfortune – and also his greatness. From out of his limitation man produces a determinate and human infinite, which envelops and liberates and overcomes the indefinite given in natural existence; this infinite might be called: the power of man, knowledge, action, love, Mind or, quite simply, the human.

The controlled sector and the uncontrolled sector

A simple law like that of falling bodies is true only for conditions often wrongly referred to as 'ideal'. It is not true for any actual body since it is true only for one falling in a vacuum. Through the operation of abstraction outside disturbances are eliminated and the natural phenomenon reduced to occurring in rigorously consolidated conditions – in terms solely of time, space and the force we call 'gravity'. This is why we can find a simple law, a mathematical relation between time and space. Such a law involves the production of a definite object. Like every product this object has a natural side and a human side, an objective content and a subjective meaning, a concrete aspect and an abstract aspect. The same holds good for geometrical space and clock-time, whose definitions enable us to determine the object 'body falling in a vacuum' and are determined by it in return. All activity, because it isolates an object in Nature, constitutes an analysis of Nature. As Engels points out in the *Dialectics of Nature*, even to crack a nut is to make an analysis. Activity separates, isolates and consolidates – and hence breaks up and kills. Yet it is seeking to attain the living, fluid reality, which it can attain only by going on trying indefinitely. Its inner contradiction forces it to transcend itself. The analysis can never be complete. Moreover, the immobilization of the product is never complete, from the side of Nature (which always reclaims the objects man has sought to abstract from it) any more than from the side of the activity, which is always moving on towards fresh determinations.

There is no such thing as a pure theoretical activity, whose exclusive purpose is an abstract dissection of the world, an abstract identification of the diverse or a complete immobilization of the fluid datum. The dialectic of activity develops into multiple relations. Deep within the world and without ever being separated from the total Praxis, it carries on a massive analysis which can never be exclusively an analysis but is also necessarily a synthesis. Activity makes manifest the relations of objects from the very fact of isolating them. The separated object is abstract, and the relation is then the concrete. But once it has been isolated the relation itself becomes abstract in respect of the object and refers to the object, to the essence of the object. Activity thus moves perpetually from the abstract to the concrete and back again. It unites, having first separated, and vice versa. It reveals relations, having first isolated elements, and vice versa.

Every product, every law, every property discovered in things therefore has a relative, approximate and provisional character – as well as an objective and concrete character.

The operation of consolidation enables us in each case to distinguish between two series of 'causes'; on the one hand there are the causes that can be easily isolated and grouped into clearly determined series relatively to the object and to the aim of the activity; on the other hand there are the 'fine' causes which, temporarily, can be ignored and seen as intrusive (the action of the air on falling bodies, for example; since such causes represent the influence of the whole of Nature on the object in question, they are always infinite in number). These 'fine' causes may subsequently become the more interesting ones, but cognition always begins by eliminating them. In this way it removes pure chance, although ready to acknowledge it later.

The essential aim of the operation of consolidation is the production of a *determinatism*. What is true of every product is equally true of every determinism: it is a creation, which does not mean an arbitrary construct. Every determinism is subtracted, by means of a practical and hence, in one sense, objective operation, from the indefinite reality of Nature, from outside disturbances, and from all effects of chance *qua* chance. Every determinism is a consolidated series. It has an objective significance and an objective reality, as well as something relative and subjective about it. Temporarily isolated, it acquires its significance from the relationships which inquiry can make manifest only by isolating it.

In the sector which man controls and which is therefore on a human scale, the activity of production as a whole – the Praxis – tends to the creation of a consolidated universe, a world made up of an immense number of determinate causal series. From this point of view, mechanism is a vast instrument whose principal function is to establish relationships subject to human control – a privileged instrument because it corresponds to the maximum success of the operation that aims at consolidating a determinism.

Thus there is something objective about mechanism and about determinism, but we must be careful not to see them as purely objective and turn them into a fatality. The determinism takes its place in the sum-total of the determinations and objectives of activity. The sum-total of determinisms constitutes a whole controlled by human activity. This sum-total, organized by the praxis and in which the unity of the real is recovered, no partial determinism being able ever wholly to shatter it, is the truly concrete.

Human activity – the Praxis – introduces oppositions into the world, which it is able to do only by accentuating those already present there in embryo.

It thus accentuates the character of those moments, aspects or properties of the real which have something distinct about them. It introduces into reality the oppositions of concrete and abstract, of necessity and chance, of causal determinism and finality. But at the same time it introduces, and produces dialectically, their unity.

Consolidation can lay down conditions for a becoming and consequently orientate it, without thereby abolishing it. For example, in a tree which we plant and tend, the objective movement is simply being protected and directed. The activity of production is wary of contradictions or objective conflicts between forces, because they may lead to the disruption of the desired consolidation. From one point of view therefore, activity takes advantage of the oppositions, accentuating them and introducing new ones, but from another point of view it is perpetually seeking to reduce and transcend the external contradiction. In general contradiction is not admitted into the products of activity except in the form of an equilibrium between opposing forces. This equilibrium leads to a temporary state of rest, then, at the required moment and in a determinate direction, a new force arrives to disturb it, one that has been carefully measured and apportioned out. Such equilibria can be observed in the theoretical constructs of mechanics or physics, as well as in the material constructs which are objects, machines, etc. In this way activity strives to consolidate the contradiction itself, to make it into an instrument and a determinism. Such an operation is feasible; it may succeed. But it is itself only relative and only true for an isolated object. It does not abolish either the dialectic of Nature or that of activity. A great many mechanist and idealist philosophers have made the mistake of raising it to be an absolute.

This is a sophism that can be avoided by passing on from consideration of the isolated product to consideration of the sum of products, from consideration of the partial activity to the movement of the total activity. Activity does not abolish contradiction, it lives on it. At the selfsame moment as it is working to reduce it, it carries it within itself; it can bring it under control and create a higher unity only by causing it to be reborn to a more profound existence.

There remains an immense sector outside man's control. Where Nature is concerned, this uncontrolled sector is, for man, fatality or brute chance. Within man himself, it is known as pure spontaneity, the unconscious, or else as his psychological or social destiny. It includes everything which human activity has so far been unable to orientate and consolidate, everything not yet 'produced' through man and for man. This means an immense part of the reality around and within man himself which has not been humanized, has not yet become an object for the Praxis. The activity of production contains within it this, the most profound of all contradictions: the agonizing opposition between man's power and his powerlessness, between the existence of one sector of reality that has been brought under control and consolidated by man, and another still in its natural state, between what makes man's life and what causes his death. At every moment man finds himself cut off from what gives him his being and what he has not yet managed to master. Thus does his essence find itself vitally threatened, finds itself being dissociated and uprooted from existence. Spiritually or materially, man dies.

This uncontrolled sector still includes, alas, almost the whole of man's natural and biological life, almost the whole of his psychological and social life. His power, which had seemed so great, suddenly appears infinitely fragile and susceptible. This sector is determined in the first place as existence, or external reality, and we can at once see that it is this existence which is the most inward and intimate.

Our attitude towards this uncontrolled sector may be to explore it by non-scientific means, to interpret it, or to project more or less arbitrarily on to it a consciousness that belongs to the controlled sector. These phenomena, of exploration, interpretation and confusion or projection, appeared as soon as the controlled sector came into existence. Exploration has been conducted by methods of literary or poetic expression; interpretation and projection have given rise to myths and religions, which are essential elements of ideologies.[1]

The primitive mind, however, contained rational elements inasmuch as it made manifest the newborn activity of production and its relation to the

[1] 'The most difficult progress of the human mind must be seen as that whereby *the fancy has subjugated the real* and in which *the continuity of the experimental sciences* has taken shape, thanks to which the human race will accomplish the dominion of thought over the planet it inhabits ... '; 'the progress of the world goes from dreams, sorcerers and auguries, from oracles and prophets, through the golden gate of artistic fancy, towards the world of a universally valid science which submits the real to human knowledge ... ' (Wilhelm Dilthey, *Gesammelte Schriften*, 2nd ed., Leipzig, 1921, p. 343.)

world. Primitive man had a more developed sense of the world's oneness (cf. the sociologists' *Mana*) than the fragmented man of our modern society. He had a muddled but vital perception of the unity of opposites. The so-called 'pre-logical' mentality (for which contradictory beings can constitute a unity) contained an element of truth not acknowledged by the ethnographers, who have judged it in terms of the rigid criteria of formal logic.

Faced by the vast sector outside man's control, this primitive mentality also includes an attitude inspired by the sector that is under control and by the consciousness appropriate to that sector. To be more exact, it extends arbitrarily the consciousness it has borrowed from the controlled sector to the un-controlled sector. The primitive mind believes it can get results by arbitrary techniques; by various forms of magic. This magic was at once an interpretation of the Praxis (primitive man was answering the ques-tion: why do we obtain such and such a result in such and such an action?), an illusory but reassur-ing extension of the power of techniques to realities both unknown and full of menace, a projection of human consciousness over the whole world, and, finally, an exploration of the unknown, poetically as well as, at times, practically, in the case of medicine, alchemy, etc. The different forms of magic and religion do not seem to have originated in one 'pre-logical mentality' (Lévy-Bruhl), nor in one original magic from which have come both religions and sciences (Frazer), nor, finally, in a religion of socio-logical origin which inspired the whole of primitive behaviour (Durkheim). The forms that are at present separated or opposed – religion, science, art – have resulted from the sociologically determined differentiation of the productive activity. Human consciousness, based on this activity but involved in the agonizing conflict between it and the world outside human control (including our physiological and sexual impulses, etc.), has sought a solution in religion, and in aesthetic expression. All these forms of activity imply a sort of indirect attempt to understand and to govern the world outside our control; scientific knowledge alone can fully realize this dominion.

But if rational elements existed in the primitive mind (elements of intuition intended to complete formal logic), then, inversely, the modern mind contains countless survivals of primitive ways of thought. The presence of the uncontrolled sector is more fascinating, more terrifying for us than it was for primitive man. Our authority is undermined, our rationality threatened. It seems that we must, at all costs and by any means, take possession of this uncontrolled sector. Mythical activity therefore persists. We are not content merely to explore this sector by methods heralding its conquest, such as certain psychological methods. Nor are we content to express it aesthetically. We still want to picture it to ourselves, to console ourselves in it or else to disarm it, to render it harmless. Hence the persistence of religion, hence too the invention of new myths and new forms of magic. We can see how difficult it is to defend Reason on purely rational grounds. Either Reason is a living power, an activity that fights to conquer both in the world and in man, a power creative of order and unity, or else it is an impotent form, destined to give way to mythical interpretations which fetishize the elements of Nature, or social products or both at once (the earth, race, State). If Reason remains purely internal, it cannot fail to succumb to external authority.

Physical determinism

Such a determinism cannot be absolute; it is relative and so approximate. It is relative to the human scale, to man's activity and to the aims of this activity. We have got constantly to extend it and make it more thorough, and link up new causal series and new fragments of the world with more far-reaching theories and objectives. We have got therefore constantly to be examining critically the degree of determinism we have attained, whose truth can be found only in later, more extensive determinations, in which the critique of this determinism is reunited with the analysis of the activity that produced it. The degree of determinism reached by a certain science can only ever be thought of therefore as a moment. In other words, every mathematical, physical, chemical, biological, etc., determinism remains always open on one side to the whole of Nature and on another side to the activity of men.

Here we meet again with the idea of the formation and consolidation of a world – our world, the one in which we are. This consolidation is relative and approximate. Our world organizes and stabilizes itself relatively, but only by opening itself and extending itself towards those realities of Nature which are on a scale other than the human. Such changes of scale pose fresh problems; the 'fine' causes move into the forefront of our investigation. The relations thus obtained are not solely relations of the part to the whole. The scientist introduces the notion of statistical determinism and formulates laws which cannot be deduced logically from the laws valid on another scale. This extension of our world has therefore been marked by the discovery of qualitatively distinct degrees of reality, whose laws are statistical in relation to the quantitative elements of which they are comprised, but, in their turn, 'atomic' in relation to higher degrees and wholes.[1]

Man's world thus appears as made up of emergences, of forms (in the plastic sense of the word) and of rhythms which are born in Nature and consolidated there relatively, even as they presuppose the Becoming in Nature. There is a human space and a human time, one side of which is in Nature and the other side independent of it. It is obvious, for example, that the human rhythms (biological, psychological and social time-scales – the time-scale of our own organism and that of the clock) determine the way in which we perceive and conceive the world and even the laws we discover in it. But human time is abstract only from one point of view (the variable t of the physicists); from another it is a fact of Nature. The laws we discover may reflect our own duration but they also have an objective meaning. To use a Hegelian formula, the tranquillity of phenomena is measured by our own rhythm, but

---

[1] In a book inspired by dialectical materialism (*A Philosophy for a Modern Man*, London, 1938), the English scientist, H. Levy, gives a lucid account of these relations, without using any mathematical apparatus. Cf. especially p. 148 et seq.

our rhythm is immersed in the rhythms of Nature, and this is why foresight and induction are possible.

We must not picture physical Nature to ourselves as a juxtapositioning or sum of determinisms external one to another. Every determinism is a product: not an abstract construct of the pure intelligence but a product of the Praxis. The sum-total of determinisms is thus a vast product of activity, an immense object: the World. This object must be understood partly in terms of Nature and partly in terms of the productive activity, which is itself a whole not absolutely separate from Nature. It is absurd, in any case, to try and picture Nature 'in itself'; in terms of determinism Nature cannot in itself be either indeterminate or determinate. 'Pure' Nature, that supremely concrete existence, is also, for us, the emptiest of abstractions. It lies on this side of all determinations, as indifference or a spontaneous Becoming (*Selbstbewegung*) as yet indeterminate for us, except in the most general and abstract laws of the dialectic. To insist on determining Nature independently of the activity which – grounded in Nature – penetrates it and 'comprehends' it, by linking its scattered elements organically together, is to pose an insoluble problem, a metaphysical problem which can be answered only by a myth. It is to try and think a World independently of the conditions under which a world can exist, independently of the Idea of the world.

The multiplicity of determinisms poses the problem of their unity. The activity of production breaks up the natural object into these determinisms, whose multiplicity is relative to the different sciences, techniques and specialized forms of knowledge. The link between them therefore is man, actual, active man. In order to be able to shape his world and overcome Nature he has been obliged to fragment his activity and the objects of his activity. He has been obliged to think of himself from different angles: as a physical, tangible and visible being; as a biological being; as dependent on mathematical calculations, etc.; and likewise the other beings of his universe. The multiplicity of determinisms reveals objective articulations of the universe, and especially the existence of degrees that have a specific reality; however, it must not be taken as an absolute. This multiplicity is only momentary, for man is one and the world around him a whole. The breaking-up of the universe into partial determinisms is constantly being overcome in life and in practice, and the dialectical unity continually re-produced. This will tend towards the higher unity to the extent that man manages to realize himself, to make of himself a specific unity enveloping Nature. Then 'the natural sciences will be subordinated to the science of man; the science of man will be subordinated to natural science; the two will form a single science'. [M]

Causal series and determinisms start from man and lead back to man. This analysis can be summed up in the formula: the physical determinism is man in Nature. This definition has to be taken in a dialectical sense; by stressing what is objective in the determinism it shows that each determinism is located within the actual activity of a natural being acting on Nature – of living man.

In order to be understood in their multiplicity – in order for their objectivity to become conceivable and, at the same time, for their unity to be determined – the sciences demand a dialectical theory of knowledge and the productive activity.

Social determinism

Marx summed up the dialectical, complex and eventful character of the historical Becoming in a striking formula: human affairs have generally progressed by their bad side. The pre-condition for most great civilizations has been slavery; revolutions and wars have been needed before limited civilizations could be destroyed and surpassed; it needed the decadence of the ancient world for its limitations from the point of view of thought and social structure to pass away. The 'bad side' gnaws away at and destroys the existent, bringing about its crisis and decline, and causing the elements of a new social reality to appear. In the first place the negative is an accidental manifestation, then it becomes a new essence, appearing to begin with in a humble, external and sporadic form. Once its originally isolated and impotent elements have increased in number, it asserts itself as a new degree of reality. Thus did the first merchants of the Middle Ages give birth to the bourgeoisie, while the first proletarians were ruined artisans, rare at first in the sixteenth century, then increasingly numerous until the new social reality, the new class appeared.

The reality of a social object is comparable to that of material objects: a social object is a product of activity, abstract from one point of view, real and concrete from another, on which we are able to act for the very reason that it is objective and resistant but not a reality given to us in its natural state.

A typical social object – the market – still exercises today a power over human beings exactly like that of the realities of the uncontrolled sector of Nature. Within it are concealed the known and the unknown, appearance and reality. It may give rise to the application of a force or a specific method of action, which fashions it.

More generally, material objects intervene in human society: they are 'goods'. They are a stimulus to social activity, to human needs and relations, but they also impose certain determinations on this activity. In particular, the scarcity of consumable objects has, right from the earliest times up until our own day (though we are now entering on the age of plenty), unleashed struggles and rivalries that have extended the natural struggle for life into the realm of the social. The objects or products of human activity do not lose this initial characteristic when they become the bearers of social relations, or when they give birth to specifically social objects such as the market. They continue to determine struggles and contradictions within man's activity. From the general rivalry emerge the struggles of certain powerful groups: the social classes.

Objects therefore determine the socio-economic Becoming and the social activity, inasmuch as they are material objects in the first place and later, properly speaking, social objects, such as commodities as a whole or the market. Political action corresponds on the human plane, and so far as social relations are concerned, to practical action on Nature. It acts through social relations as well as on them; it intervenes in conflicts and makes use of the conflicting forces. At no time in history have there been absolute dividing-lines between epochs, civilizations or classes. The socio-economic movement has always been a complex one. Political action has constantly striven to contain this movement within determinate forms and, to this end, to eliminate disruptive elements. It has always tried to intervene in order to carve 'consolidated' structures out of the spontaneous Becoming: the forms of Government, which are products of action being applied to social relations by utilizing opposed forces, and hence always applied for the benefit of the more powerful of these forces. But here again, these attempts have, right up until our own day, caused ever more profound contradictions to appear and have prepared the way for the emergence of new forces and forms.

This analysis too can be summed up in a formula: the social determinism is Nature in man. The social determinism in fact is what makes a specifically human activity possible; it conditions it, but it also limits it. The social determinism makes man's freedom possible, yet it is also opposed to it. It originates in natural objectivity, which is extended into the objectivity of Fetishes and the specific objectivity of social relations. It originates also in natural determinations: the scarcity of goods, the natural struggle for life. Social realities and social objects appear as the consequence of spontaneous processes comparable to those revealed by the sciences of Nature: as the statistical results of elementary phenomena.

The social determinism is thus the inhuman within the human, the continuation into the human of natural conflicts and biological realities. It is man as yet unrealized: Nature in man.

The total man

Man originates as a humble fragment of Nature, the feeblest and nakedest of all biological beings. But this feeblest of beings boldly joins battle; he becomes an 'essence' separated from natural existence, at once vulnerable but powerful. This Separation is fundamental; man no longer is or can be Nature; yet he is only in and by virtue of Nature. This contradiction is reproduced and grows more profound during the actual process which must lead to man overcoming it. Man is creative activity; he produces himself through his activity. He produces himself, yet he is not what he produces. Bit by bit his activity brings Nature under control, but only for his mastery to turn against him, to take on the characteristics of an external nature and involve him in the social determinism which inflicts terrible suffering on him. Man is not this determinism – and yet without it he is nothing. In the first place the human exists only in and by virtue of the inhuman. Not only does man depend on Nature, but he is the feeblest element even of society. Man opposes the biological brutality to which he is subject no less brutally: in Law, Morality and Religion.

Man is thus profoundly divided, but it is only by virtue of this division that he can form himself. To start with, it is only a contradiction between himself and Nature. Within this contradiction the two terms act on one another reciprocally, the characteristics of one pass over into the other; after every resolution the contradiction reappears in a form all the more profound and dramatic because the unity that had been attained was a higher and more conscious one.

Hitherto, those activities which actually overcome the natural forms of antagonism (the Praxis, thought, Mind which involves a certain immanent unity and dominates the external world) have served only to worsen man's divisions and conflicts and make him feel them more keenly.

It still seems that the human does not exist, that it is only an illusion or a consolation. Yet man is already in existence; he is made manifest to us as soon as we take into account human activity as a whole and stop seeing each object, event and individual in accordance with their ephemeral particularities. In the first place man's essence is an abstract possibility: an eternal split or separation. It seems as if this essence has, as yet, only an ideal, metaphysical existence. But each problem posed by a contradiction calls for its solution, moves towards that solution, determines an activity that will transcend it and thus posits a fresh degree of actuality for the human essence. Each time a contradiction is resolved, living man draws closer to that essence; it is as if the latter were the immanent driving force of history and of the dramatic movement of human affairs. Discovery and creation converge: the human is at once created (produced) and discovered.

Idealism isolates that part of man which emerges gradually, considering it 'in itself', independent of the conditions of its existence, as if it had 'succeeded' in advance – for all eternity. In this way idealism makes the birth of man seem without drama.

Man is born and realizes himself in that which is 'other' in relation to himself, in that which denies him and which he denies, and yet which is intimately joined to him: Nature. He is merged with Nature yet gradually acquires authority over it, creating for himself a human nature.

As commonly used this term has become deceptively familiar and its true meaning has been concealed. Nature becomes human; around and within man it becomes a world, an organized experience. And man becomes nature, a concrete existence, a power. Human labour humanizes man's natural environment. And Nature is internalized by man and becomes a rational life-force, an instinctive energy freed from the limitations of natural and passive instinct. Human nature is a unity, an exchange of Being, a transcending of the Separation.

Labour – economic production – is not an end in itself. 'The essential outcome of production ... is the existence of man.' [M]

Nature is the inorganic body of man ... Man lives off Nature, which means to say: Nature is his body, with which he must remain linked by a constant process in order not to die. That man's physical and spiritual life should be in touch with Nature, merely means that Nature is in touch with itself, for man is part of Nature ... But it is in the elaboration of the world of objects that man affirms himself as a specific being. This production is the active life of his species, thanks to which Nature appears as his handiwork and his reality. The object of labour is therefore objectification and the specific life of man – in so far as he duplicates himself, not intellectually, as in consciousness, but really, in action, and contemplates himself in a world created by him ... [M]

Social history is the history of man's appropriation of Nature and of his own nature. Social labour and economic activity are the means of this appropriation, essential moments of the human essence – once they have been brought under control and integrated by this essence. In themselves they are not this essence. Economic man has got to be transcended, so that the freedom of the total man can be made manifest: 'Man appropriates to himself his multiple essence (*Allseitiges*) ... inasmuch as he is total man.' [M]

The total movement is broken up by action and by thought. This separation cannot be absolute, but it does have a relative reality grounded on man's struggle against Nature. Physical determinism depends on man acting in and on Nature. Social determinism extends Nature into man. Human Nature resolves these conflicts, deploys a higher unity and transcends the determinisms by organizing them. Just like Nature seen in its totality, human nature is spontaneity (*Selbstbewegung*), but an organized and rational one. The total man is 'all Nature'; within him he contains all the energies of matter and of life, and the whole past and future of the world; but he transforms Nature into will and freedom.

Products and the forces of production are the 'other' of this total man, in which he may be destroyed. The independence of economic forces – the destiny of modern man – must be understood and brought under control. As soon as the objectivity of the social process is defined as such, it is already on the way to being transcended. It is united with the activity of the active and already objective human subject, and supplies him with a new objective content; it is 'subjectified' in him, but only so that a more objective human activity can arise, which can take itself more effectively as the object of an action, 'produce' itself more rationally and be its own conscious creation.

The various forms of destiny have always been this 'other' of man. History has been irreparably bloody and tragic too in so far as no destiny can be justified in respect of those who endure it, but only by the human future which all forms of destiny at once prepare for and paralyse. Yet history has not been a meaningless chaos of anecdotes and acts of violence. Such a view of history denies history, which can exist as such only by virtue of its living subject, the total man who forms himself through history.

Man has not yet been born, he is still in the throes of childbirth; as unity and resolution he is hardly even a presentiment. As yet he is only in and through his opposite: the inhuman within him. As yet, he is dispersed throughout the multiple activities and specialized forms of production into which reality and the new-born consciousness of human nature are broken up. As yet, he is conscious of himself only in what is other than himself: in ideologies.

Once the creative activity has become diversified social man continues to discover himself in the results of his action, but the products invested with consciousness cease to be immediate, as they are for primitive man or for children. They become social and abstract. A new sort of product appears: spiritual products; and henceforward there are three degrees of external yet essential production: material products, social objects properly so called and spiritual products. From one point of view these last are objects, they are external to the consciousness of human individuals. In another sense they depend strictly on the activity in a given social framework at a particular moment of history. These ideologies express both the global activity of social groups, the level attained by their practical power and the breaking-up of the world and of consciousness into fragmentary activities. They disguise the true relations. The activity that seeks to become conscious of itself in them is uprooted from itself and, so to speak, carried out of itself. Ideological representations transpose the human on to the plane of things, of external substances: gods, destinies, absolute metaphysical truth. These spiritual things are superimposed on material things, with which they have no conscious relationship, until men are made to lose all awareness of their own creative activity. The objectivity of spiritual products contains an element of illusion, but this appearance is turned into a reality: men believe that their social representations have a transcendent origin and organize themselves accordingly, as this belief is taken over and exploited politically. Theoretical alienation thus becomes practical alienation, by reacting on the praxis. Myths and Fetishes seem to be endowed with a real power – the power that men have in fact conferred on them and which is nothing but their own power being turned against them.

In another sense, these products contain a truth. They express concrete human life by transposing it. They become the elements of ways of life or cultures which have always had a partial validity and certain of which (especially Greek life and culture) can perhaps be integrated into the modern world once this has been organized and renewed. In general, such

ways of life resulted from the repetition and accu-
mulation of the humblest actions of practical
life. History displays, however, in most great
civilizations, a distressing contradiction between the
magnificence of ideological justifications, costumes
and words, and the monotony of everyday gestures.
Only the future will be able to resolve this form of
contradiction between consciousness and reality.

Ideologies are effective essentially because people
believe in them; but, bit by bit, consciousness with-
draws from such products, and reconquers itself
through reflection and through the development of
a real dominion over the world. All ideologies have
been transcended in history, after a greater or lesser
period of 'unhappy consciousness'. Thought and the
human reality are formed through ideologies, but
only by transcending them and freeing themselves
from them, so that they can finally posit themselves
as real activities.

Even today, at a time when his dominion over
Nature is already great, living man is more than ever
the victim of the Fetishes he himself has raised up,
those strange existences, both abstract and real,
brutally material yet clad in ideologies that are
alluring and sometimes even bewitching. A new consciousness is needed, tenacious, rational and scepti-
cal, in order that these Fetishes should be unmasked
and in order that the reason should not be swept
away out of control. Dialectical materialism seeks
to be the expression and the organ of this
consciousness.

Living men still do not fully understand their
essence and their true greatness. The analysis of the
production of man by himself shows that all the

philosophical definitions of man's essence correspond to moments of that production. The term 'production' is essential, because it contains the other terms and explains them: because it contains and presupposes in man Nature, action and knowledge. It is a word frequently understood very trivially, because it is used in its most limited sense, but it signifies the whole greatness of man. Its truth is not yet self-evident because even today human life is not produced consciously and does not comprehend its own production. It moves within Fetishism, as a mode of existence and of consciousness.

> The object produced by labour ... is opposed to man as an alien being, as an independent power. Just as, in religion, the spontaneous activity of the fancy, of the brain and the human heart, acts on the individual in a way that is independent of him, as an alien activity, either divine or diabolical, so the activity of the producer is not his own spontaneous activity ... His vital activity, the productive life of man, appears to him only as a means, in order to satisfy a need: the physical need to survive ... Life itself appears only as a means ... ' [M]

'All production is an appropriation of Nature by the individual, within and by means of a social form.' [KPO] To say that today man's essence is still 'alienated' means above all that the forms of our society do not permit this appropriation of Nature by the individual. What ought (in ethical terms) to be an 'end in itself' is still only a means: man's creative activity, his essence, his individuality.

The present situation is intolerable because the

human reality is more profoundly dissociated than ever. Today it seems as if all the possible varieties of division, dispersion and contradiction have come to-gether, have converged to cause man untold suffer-ing. The reality of the human is imperilled, it is grow-ing blurred in our minds and it is threatened in its concrete existence.

A time has come 'when everything that men had looked on as inalienable has become an object of exchange or of barter, and can be alienated'. Virtue and conscience, love and knowledge, which had hitherto been passed on generously, as a gift, are now commercialized. 'This is the age of general corrup-tion, of universal venality.' [MP] The need for money is the one true need 'engendered by political economy', with the result that 'the quantity of money is becoming more and more the one essential quality of man'. This alienation gives rise, sometimes with-in the selfsame individuals, both to refined and artificial forms of greed and to a bestial simplification of their needs. Man sinks lower than the animals; he enters into solitude. He sometimes goes so far as to lose even the desire for true commerce with his fellows. The whole of life is, for him, an alien power which he feels 'slipping through his fingers'. The social essence is inhuman, it is quite simply money. It is thus precisely an economic essence: 'My means of subsistence are those of someone else. Whatever is the object of my desire is the inaccessible possession of someone else. Everything is other than itself; even my activity is other. In the end – and this is also true for the capitalist – an inhuman power reigns over the whole.' [MP] The inhuman is precisely this predominance of the economic: the essence of man has been handed over to a thing, to money, to the Fetish. (It is fairly symptomatic of the present reversal of values that Marx should have been accused of an 'absolute economicism', whereas the essential aim of his philosophy is to transcend economic man.)

As an individual, the capitalist is a man 'deprived' of everything except money. But the non-capitalist experiences a more brutal privation, his social content and vital substance being external in relation to the individual. He lacks money, which is the sole meaning of a social life based on profit. The human man is unthinkable outside a community. All social structures have defined a certain unity. However, whenever a community is rent by internal conflicts, whether latent or ostensible, it ceases to be a true community. Man reverts to being an animal for man, and the human is then alienated as well as the human community.

The present multiform alienation of man and of the community is grounded in the inhuman situation of certain social groups, the most important of which is the modern proletariat. This social group is excluded from the community, or else admitted to it only in appearance, verbally – so that it can be exploited politically. Neither in its material nor in its spiritual condition does it share in the community, and whenever it takes action in order to do so its enemies say that it is destroying the community!

In a social structure based on the private ownership of the principal means of production, the proletariat is merely one instrument amongst many, an 'appendage of the machine'. [Man] The modern worker has to sell his labour-power, he becomes a commodity, a thing amongst other things. Labour is an external power, it 'is exercised over the individual as over a thing'. [K III]

> The more the worker produces by his labour [Marx had already written in 1844], the more powerful the alien world of objects he creates opposite him becomes, and the more impoverished his inner world ... His labour is external to the labourer; he does not affirm himself in his labour but denies himself, and feels unhappy ... He feels himself only outside of his labour; his labour therefore is not the satisfaction of a need but only a means of satisfying needs independent of him ... The activity of the labourer therefore is not his auto-activity. It belongs to another, it is the loss of himself. As a result, the man who works no longer feels free except in his animal functions: eating, drinking, breeding. In his human functions he no longer feels himself to be anything but an animal. True, eating, drinking and breeding are also authentically human functions. But in the abstraction that separates them from the other spheres of activity and turns them into an end, they become animal ... This relation is that of the labourer and of his own activity inasmuch as it is alien to him. [M]

The producers are thus (both as individuals and as a group) separated from and deprived of the goods they have created. The producers as a whole do not receive the material products as a whole in order to consume them. The economic consequence of this is the relative surplus-production which turns the abundance that is today a possibility into a privation – into a crisis, into political and economic conflicts.

The life of the human community is broken up. Creative activity becomes a means for the individual, who is thus separated from the community. In particular, the community is only a means for the individuals possessing the means of production.

In this way alienation extends over the whole of life, and the individual cannot escape from it. Whenever he tries to free himself he isolates himself in himself, which is nothing more nor less than an acute form of alienation. The human essence results from the totality of the social process. The individual can attain it only if he has a rational and coherent relationship with the community; he must neither separate himself from the community nor lose himself in it. However, in our own society, in which relations appear to have been inverted, the individual may believe that he is realizing himself by isolating himself, in which case he is more profoundly 'deprived' still, and cut off from his base, from his social roots. He can grasp himself only as a theoretical abstraction (as soul, inner life, ideal) or as a biological being (body, sexual desire). He fosters and reproduces within himself, in a more severe form, the dissociation of the community. The contradiction within him is multiform: between the unconscious and consciousness, between the natural and the human, between the social and the individual, between instinct and rationality, between content and form – between practice and theory.

The proletariat is the concrete element of this society, its practical aspect. Through its labour it is in constant contact with the materiality and resistance of things, with the contradictions of given existence. Dialectical materialism has taken shape as an expression of the proletariat, although it transcends the limitations of the proletarian condition precisely by becoming aware of them, in the name of philosophical culture, of economic science and of all the hopes of social reformers. The proletariat therefore possesses certain essential elements of the human. On the other hand, the bourgeoisie possesses certain other equally essential elements: rationality and culture. These last, simply because they have become separated from the first, have become abstract and formal. The community of man has been replaced by the more or less concealed exercise of violence over an essential part of man – by the infinite dispersion into individualism and the rivalry of competing individuals. This dispersion has manifested itself even within individuality itself; the concrete, practical or natural element has become separated from the rational or cultural one. Rationality brings the concrete content under control by violence; the spiritual powers, deprived of a content, function abstractly. The cultured individual has become the 'theoretical man' described by Nietzsche.

The material and spiritual dissociation of our society can only get worse. It has entered necessarily into its decline (as is confirmed by the specifically economic analysis). To put an end to this situation we have got to transcend the social structure which subordinates one class to another and subjects one profound element of the human reality to another, because these human elements are wielded by conflicting groups. We have got to overcome an economic organization in which the proletariat is only an instrument of production, and in which, correspondingly, the reality of production is underestimated. In particular, in order to resolve the opposition between the individual and the social, in order to discover the connection and unity between the elements of the content, we have got to become fully conscious of the praxis. Since the limitations of our consciousness are themselves grounded in a certain praxis (that of our own economic and social structure), this must be overcome so that we can create a new praxis, a coherent, 'planned' one.

We may in fact be close to achieving the human essence in this extreme dispersion and contradiction, in our material and our spiritual plight. This essence will attain a richer unity for having been alienated in such a multiplicity; so profound are the contradictions that they make a unity imperative.

In this way, in materialist humanism, the notions of the idealist become more precise: the *en-soi* and the *pour-soi*, the seed and the fulfilment, alienation and the transcending, object and subject, essence and existence. By starting from an analysis of the Praxis, it is possible to show how the moments of the activity come into being, as well as the categories of thought and of action, and the different spheres of knowledge. The dialectical notion of alienation dominates and epitomizes this description of man in his Becoming. It takes account both of the present drama and the historical drama of the human. It provides the final significance of the Praxis. Conversely, the analysis of the Praxis confers a positive character on this notion.

The total man is both the subject and the object of the Becoming. He is the living subject who is opposed to the object and surmounts this opposition. He is the subject who is broken up into partial activities and scattered determinations and who surmounts this dispersion. He is the subject of action, as well as its final object, its product even if it does seem to produce external objects. The total man is the living subject-object, who is first of all torn asunder, dissociated and chained to necessity and abstraction. Through this tearing apart, he moves towards freedom; he becomes Nature, but free. He becomes a totality, like Nature, but by bringing it under control. The total man is 'de-alienated' man.

A practical and materialist philosophy cannot allow itself to offer a transcendent ideal; its ideal must be a function of reality. It must have its roots in this reality, and exist there already, as a potentiality. The ideal of the total man satisfies this requirement. Moreover, the reality of what is humanly possible can be determined scientifically, by specifically economic or sociological investigation.

Human alienation will end with 'the return of man to himself', that is to say in the unity of all the elements of the human. This 'perfect naturalism' coincides with humanism. It will create the human man by preserving the entire content of his evolution. 'This is the true end of the quarrel between existence and essence, between objectification and the affirmation of self, between freedom and necessity, between the individual and the species. It resolves the mystery of history and knows that it resolves it.'[1]

This organization of the human community will not put an end to history but rather to man's 'prehistory', his 'natural history', before he became fully

[1] Marx-Engels Archiv, III.

differentiated from the animals. It will inaugurate the era of an authentic humanity, in which man will control his own destiny and try at last to resolve the specifically human problems: those of happiness, knowledge, love and death. He will have been freed from the conditions that made these problems insoluble. For example, biological inequality between individuals is an undeniable fact, but it is monstrous to make use of this fact, or accentuate it so as to profit from it. In a human society such problems will be posed and investigated with a view to solving them practically. Concrete social equality will not abolish natural inequalities but, on the contrary, will display them, by giving individual talents the opportunity of fulfilling themselves. After which the war must be carried to the biological element, in order to bring that under control, and in order to discover and conquer the necessities stemming from heredity, geographical or racial inevitability, etc.

As thus defined, humanism has a quantitative aspect: it is based on the development of the forces of production. It also has a qualitative aspect. Every human community has a quality or style. Human communities and styles exist already: as nations, cultures and traditions. Total humanism does not aim to destroy these communities but, on the contrary, to free them from their restrictions, to enrich them so that they tend towards a concrete universality without losing anything of their reality. The total movement has got to be carried on, by developing and enveloping the content of the present.

For such a humanism, the supreme instance is not society, but the total man. The total man is a free individual in a free community. He is an individuality which has blossomed into the limitless variety of possible individualities.

But this is not the *inevitable* outcome of human prehistory, it cannot be produced by economic fatalism, nor by some mysterious finality of history, nor by a decree of 'society'. The living individuals acting on its behalf may be defeated. Humanity may enter into confusion and chaos. The solution is indicated within the total movement; it gives a direction to our view of the future, to our activities and our consciousness, it does not abolish them. How could economic and social automatism be brought to an end automatically?

Art has always involved a tension, a striving towards a total act. In music a partial element of our sense-awareness – sound – tends to become coextensive with the content of consciousness: as rhythm, movement, passion, eroticism or spirituality. The same applies in painting with the visual element. The art of vanished epochs, whose social structure no longer has any practical significance for us, remains of irreplaceable value. In the most mystical poetry we can also find certain premonitions of this total act, which has been called the Divine or the Superhuman, and has always been projected outside man in the name of cosmic feelings both ardent and obscure. Hitherto the striving for oneness has nearly always been manifested in alienation. Man was hoping to find unity and reconciliation with himself, peace of mind and salvation, in some external belief. The unity of man with the community was sought for in religious ritual or moral imperatives. The unity of man with the universe seemed to have been attained in certain moments of ecstatic communion in which the consciousness emerged from itself, and whose intensity was possible only as the price of a lengthy self-discipline. Such flights did not provide a true solution. The moment of conversion, of communion or ecstasy, having passed, the human being came back to his wretchedness, more profoundly torn and more desperate than ever: his being was outside the human. Of all these strivings it is art which has retained the greatest value for us.

The idea of the total man extends these strivings, but on to a positive and effectual plane. It contains within it the highest values of the past, especially art, as being a productive form of labour freed from the characteristics of alienation, and as being a unity of the product and the producer, of the individual and the social, of natural Being and the human being.

This supreme ideal provides the Becoming with a meaning because it is involved in the Becoming itself. The total man is the Idea, that idea which idealism reduced one-sidedly to the theoretical activity, and which it thought of as outside life, ready-made in the absolute.

Ultimately, the total act would be supremely individualized as well as co-extensive with the life-force, supremely rational as well as supremely spontaneous. Yet, immersed in the rhythms of Nature, it would be a unique presence.

But the highest, the most profoundly human and total consciousness, can still only accentuate the first and most profound of contradictions: that between Being and Nothingness, or between life and death. No doubt man will never be able finally to conquer death and possess his being without fear of losing it. But man fights against death; the human man is the one who has accepted the challenge. Nor is it only in front of him that he finds the ungraspable power of Nothingness, for death has accomplices amongst men. The human man rejects all complicity with death, but pledges himself thereby to the struggle against death's accomplices.

The perishable individual has, in his Ego, more than himself: he has man, mind and Being. The human man will seek to hand on and perpetuate this Being, to make it more extensive and more profound, to 'participate' in Being to the utmost. In this way he fights against death in himself.

The 'theoretical man' must thus pledge himself to recover, elucidate and transcend a vast human reality. He must open his abstract, theoretical and formal Ego to the World. The new philosophy depends on a real act and on an exigency, not on a postulate, an abstract alternative, an arbitrarily chosen value or a fiction. Its task is to 'make effective' the connections implicit between all the elements and aspects of the content of the human consciousness and Being. In this quest, the only criterion is a practical one: to eliminate whatever arrests the movement, whatever separates and dissociates, whatever hinders the Transcending.

Towards the total content

The philosophical mind and action which are not content with a merely formal position or a wholly theoretical outlook, can seek to avoid the hiatus between form and content by grasping immediately a certain concrete content. But if the move to grasp a partial content is restricted to this one element of the real, it necessarily erects it into an absolute; it turns it into a fetishized form. For example, we may grasp as a content: the psychological reality of the individual; the national community; the spiritual reality of man; the human need for unity and reality. Each of these 'moments' of the real, once isolated and hypostatized, becomes the negator of the other moments and then the negator of itself. Limited and transposed into a form, the content becomes oppressive and destructive of its own reality. Thus nationalism becomes the enemy of national realities, liberalism allows liberty to perish, spiritualism becomes the adversary of the living spirit and individualism that of the concrete individual, while 'totalitarianism' is opposed to the total realization of man.

Philosophically, to proceed thus turns a partial truth into an error precisely by positing it in the absolute. It creates a meta-something. Racialism is a meta-biology, the theory of nationalism a meta-history or meta-sociology. Such a procedure involves all the risks of metaphysics. By rejecting a part of the content it gives sanction to and aggravates the dispersion of the elements of the real. It ignores the contribution of other spheres, and thus appears as a specialized or partisan procedure. It expresses a defence mechanism of the individual or of his group, rather than a mind directed towards the solution.

For the mind that is truly anxious to resolve these problems only one way lies open: it must strive to grasp the total content. It is this striving which will define the philosophical life.

Paris, 1938

SELECTED BIBLIOGRAPHY

A list of the principal works of Henri Lefebvre,
with the dates of their first appearance

LE MATÉRIALISME DIALECTIQUE (Alcan, Paris, 1939)

L'EXISTENTIALISME (Sagittaire, Paris, 1946)

LE MARXISME (Collection 'Que sais-je?', Presses Universitaires de France, Paris, 1948)

CONTRIBUTION À L'ESTHÉTIQUE (Éditions Sociales, Paris, 1953)

LES PROBLÈMES ACTUELS DU MARXISME (Collection 'Initiation Philosophique', Presses Universitaires de France, Paris, 1958)

LA SOMME ET LE RESTE (Éditions La Nef de Paris, Paris, 1959)

INTRODUCTION À LA MODERNITÉ (Éditions de Minuit, Paris, 1962)

LA VALLÉE DE CAMPAN (Presses Universitaires de France, Paris, 1963)

LA PROCLAMATION DE LA COMMUNE (Collection 'Les 30 journées qui ont fait la France', Gallimard, Paris, 1965)

MÉTAPHILOSOPHIE (Éditions de Minuit, Paris, 1965)

LE LANGAGE ET LA SOCIÉTÉ (Collection 'Idées', Gallimard, Paris, 1966)

POSITION: CONTRE LES TECHNOCRATES (Gonthier, Paris, 1967)

In addition, M. Lefebvre has been responsible for a number of editions, selections and commentaries (some in collaboration with Norbert Guterman) on the following writers: Marx, Hegel, Lenin, Nietzsche, Descartes, Pascal, Diderot, de Musset and Rabelais.

THE AUTHOR

Henri Lefebvre was born in 1901. At eighteen he already held a philosophy degree. His career as a college teacher was cut short by the Second World War and he served in the Resistance from 1942 to 1944. At the Liberation, he held a responsible position in the Radiodiffusion Française and in 1948 was appointed *chargé de cours* in France's unique research establishment, the Centre National de la Recherche Scientifique. In 1954 he obtained his *doctorat d'État* with a thesis on the economy of French peasant life. Six years later he was made *maître de recherches* at the C.N.R.S. and was then elected to the Chair of Sociology at the University of Strasbourg in 1960. Today, Henri Lefebvre is professor at the Faculty of Letters and Human Sciences of Nanterre (University of Paris); *chargé de cours* at the École Pratique des Hautes Études in Paris; Director of a research group within the C.N.R.S. and Director of the Institute of Urban Sociology.

CAPE EDITIONS

1 The Scope of Anthropology, Claude Lévi-Strauss
2 Call Me Ishmael, Charles Olson
3 Writing Degree Zero, Roland Barthes
4 Elements of Semiology, Roland Barthes
5 I Wanted to Write a Poem, William Carlos Williams
6 The Memorandum, Václav Havel
7 Selected Poems, Nazim Hikmet
8 Lichtenberg: Aphorisms & Letters
9 Tango, Slawomir Mrozek
10 On Love ... Aspects of a Single Theme, José Ortega y Gasset
11 Manhood, Michel Leiris
12 Bees: Their Vision, Chemical Senses, and Language, Karl von Frisch
13 Lunar Caustic, Malcolm Lowry
14 Twenty Prose Poems, Charles Baudelaire
15 Journeys, Günter Eich
16 A Close Watch on the Trains, Bohumil Hrabal
17 Mayan Letters, Charles Olson
18 The Courtship Habits of the Great Crested Grebe, Julian Huxley
19 The Supermale, Alfred Jarry
20 Poems & Antipoems, Nicanor Parra
21 In Praise of Krishna: Songs from the Bengali
22 History Will Absolve Me, Fidel Castro
23 Selected Poems, Georg Trakl
24 Selected Poems, Yves Bonnefoy
25 Ferdinand, Louis Zukofsky
26 The Recluse, Adalbert Stifter
27 Dialectical Materialism, Henri Lefebvre
29 Soul on Ice, Eldridge Cleaver
30 The Human Sciences and Philosophy, Lucien Goldmann
31 Selected Poems, André Breton
32 Soap, Francis Ponge
33 Histoire Extraordinaire, Michel Butor
34 Conversations with Claude Lévi-Strauss, G. Charbonnier
35 An Absence, Uwe Johnson
36 A Critique of Pure Tolerance, Robert Paul Wolff, Barrington Moore Jr, Herbert Marcuse
37 The Garden Party, Václav Havel
38 Twenty Love Poems, Pablo Neruda
39 Genesis as Myth and Other Essays, Edmund Leach